Shakesperience

An Approach to Performing Shakespeare

By

Jack K. Wann

Published by Northwestern State University Press
Don Sepulvado, Director
Neill Cameron, Editor

Northwestern State University of Louisiana, 71497

ISBN: 0-91789822-2

Cover Image: Photography of the author appearing as Sir John
Falstaff in Horse Cave Theatre's 1985 production of William
Shakespeare's <u>Henry IV, Part I</u>, Warren Hammack Producer/Director.

To Regan Wann

PREFACE

This book provides a practical and step-by-step approach to performing Shakespeare WITHOUT any digression into Life and Times, Theories of Authorship, and all the many related topics that are often contained in texts on Shakespearean acting. It is designed for student actors at an introductory level with limited experience acting in verse.

The goal is simple. Get the actors "on their feet" and immersed in the material as quickly as possible, armed with tools that will make their "Shakesperience" not only valuable, but also joyful.

Contents

WHY ANOTHER BOOK ON SHAKESPEARE?

The word Shakespeare connotes more than
any other man's name that ever was written
or spoken upon earth.
> — Algernon Charles Swinburne

The dramatic work of William Shakespeare is, not to waste time or to mince words, the BEST our language has to offer. It was created for working theatre artists by a fellow traveller. The man wrote FOR the theatre, and his art is not complete until it comes alive in performance. Although it cannot be denied that the author was a genius and that his work would rank as great literature whether bound in leather on library shelves or performed in theatres all over the world, it is only at that moment when the living artist and the text meld together that we feel a true "Shakesperience."

Shakespeare's philosophical and psychological insights, revealing a deep and compassionate understanding of the human condition, appeal to the actor on every level. When this is joined with his technical skill as a practitioner in the theatre, we have at our disposal a virtual gold mine of dramatic potential.

Composed of bold strokes and energetically painted on a broad canvas, the sense of the uniquely vital and "risky" afford the actor welcome challenges found nowhere else. The drive of the language comes from writing for a society that loved words—newly coined words, freshly minted words, words to savor, and words with which to make love, debate, and banter. This love of words provides the contemporary performing artist with a wonderful laboratory for articulation and diction plus opportunities for utilizing the punch of operative words, inflection, scansion, gesture, facial expression, parallelisms, effective antecedents, antitheses, and other literary and actor's "devices." Many of these devices will be major topics in the pages that follow.

After many years of training young artists in university courses, I have become totally convinced that you cannot really TEACH Shakespeare. I am equally convinced, however, that it can be LEARNED, primarily through exposure and immersion. Teachers and students working together can provide this combination, and it is to that end that this book is dedicated.

HOW WILL THIS BOOK BE DIFFERENT OR UNIQUELY HELPFUL TO THE BEGINNING SHAKESPEAREAN ACTOR?

> Shakespeare...has been mutilated, mugged
> and masticated. He has been taken to the
> heights by some of our greatest actors, and
> to the depths by others. He has been translated,
> truncated, humiliated and musicalized. He has been
> quoted, quartered and pulverized; butchered, bullied
> and bashed beyond all recognition; misquoted and
> mismanaged; played by men, women and children
> whenever the fancy took them. He has challenged us
> all and won hands down. He has made a fool of most
> of us at one time or another. There he stands, finger
> on cheek, quizzical, slightly bewildered, but passing
> the baton through century after century.
>
> — Laurence Olivier

Most actors venture into their first experiences with Shakespeare with apprehension. They feel they lack much of what they have observed in the classical actors they hold in high regard— the magnificent voices,the facility for acting in verse, the graceful movement, the skills with weapons, the comfort in exotic costume elements and, most important, the intellectual and emotional understanding of the archaic texts. But, these are skills that can be learned through reading, training, and exercise. They are not gifts delivered miraculously from on high. This book will provide a springboard from which the inexperienced actor can advance to new and higher levels of comprehension and efficiency with Shakespearean text and the intellectual, emotional, and physical demands required of the plays.

The text is divided into fourteen units. Each will address a particular set of issues, problems, or concepts relative to the acting of Shakespeare in the form of a kind of classroom "lecture," followed by one or more acting exercises related to the topic. From the outset the student actors are expected to be "on their feet," experiencing Shakespeare—not just reading about him. This is the "Shakesperience" of the title and the ultimate goal of the book.

So, let's do some Shakespeare!

Unit One

SHAKESPEARE ON THE PAGE

Acting in Verse or "It's Greek to me!"

When the student-actor first looks at Shakespeare on the page, he sees a word arrangement and a vocabulary foreign to that which he has used on stage before. He is faced with convoluted word order (subjects and verbs often distant from one another) and antiquated forms that are unfamiliar at best. The first thing you must learn to do is to PAY NO ATTENTION TO THAT ARRANGEMENT ON THE PAGE. The line arrangement must never be taken as an invitation for pauses or stops. Breaks in reading Shakespeare do not come at the end of lines, but at the ends of thoughts. Use only the punctuation as a guide, and avoid "sing-songy" recitations.The actor should begin all acting work by seeking the SENSE of the monologue or scene.*

> Most (people) have this notion that classical
> culture has to be good for you....I have directed
> some of these plays several times, and I still
> don't understand them. But you're not meant to
> UNDERSTAND Shakespeare. Everyone thinks
> that at the end of an art experience they have
> to answer twenty questions and get nineteen right.
> No! What matters is your own personal interaction
> with the play....It's like life. There's enough there
> for everyone to find something for themselves.
> —Peter Sellars

*Note: There are many methods of approaching Shakespeare. This book supports no "enlightened path" to the text and may even prove contradictory to other views. It simply suggests a way for the student-actor to get started. With study and research, he will find many "paths," all of which may ultimately prove useful.

SIMPLE COMMUNICATION MUST COME FIRST! The Shakespearean actor must communicate by finding ways to make the language his own. Both verse and prose must appear to come from within on a personal and dynamic level. Unfortunately, many students have suffered the slings and arrows of negative experiences with Shakespeare in their academic pasts and have come to regard the work as distant from their own lives. In some ways they view it as frozen and museum-like in form and content, so that a natural vocal presentation is difficult.

It is a major hurdle for many young performers to realize that the fundamental rules for acting any accessible and familiar material apply equally to Shakespearean text. The challenges of acting in verse involve precisely the same basic skills and techniques as acting in modern prose.

In Shakespeare, as in any acting endeavor, the actor must begin with a premise that he "knows something the audience doesn't know....and THIS is what it is." In this way, addressing a Shakespearean audience for the first time, he may feel free to play intentions ("objectives," "motivations," "wants," or "needs"— feel free to use your actor terminology) in the same way that he might rehearse and perform any familiar material. Once he has determined what it is he "knows" — his acting intention, or what he is "fighting for" (directors of Shakespeare might refer to this as his "argument") — he is then able to DO something about the obstacles that are in the way of the realization of his objective. The result is the dramatic CONFLICT from which all acting potential springs. Since most current theorists agree that acting is "doing," what you decide to "do" about a situation becomes the catalyst for all acting choices and a major guide to the sense of the text. In Shakespeare, the WORDS tell you what to do. The language holds the key to all decisions. "This above all," trust the text!

With dedicated application of his customary acting technique, the student actor will soon see the words functioning much like notes in a superior piece of music, and he will find the rhythm of the lines of both rhymed and blank verse becoming "friendlier." Shakespeare, the consummate theatre artist, employed his verse to clarify and complement the moods, needs, and desires of his characters.The student will also come to welcome the "heartbeat" of the lines from a purely technical perspective. Since the iambic pentameter of much of Shakespeare's text is the verse form closest to the human pulse, the beats themselves provide anchor points and support for the memorization of roles. (Remember, Shakespeare's acting companies were often required to perform as many as sixty roles in a single season. Any aids to memorization would have been greatly appreciated.)

Even as verse is used today to help our children remember important occasions (for example, "30 days hath September, April, June and November"), so Shakespeare used the meter of his lines to provide mnemonic "cues" for members of the often overextended professional troupes rehearsing in three-week intervals. Striving for both beauty and dynamics in the readings, Shakespearean actors must meet the requirements of the meter without resorting to extremes like omitting "beats" or pounding the verse into submission. The development of the ability to move between verse and prose while sustaining character implications proves an additional demand placed upon the actor doing Shakespeare.

The inexperienced young actor may see the plays as collections of poems. This is certainly not the case. Sometimes a preferred practice is to encourage actors to think of the lines NOT as poetry, but as the HEIGHTENED LANGUAGE needed for extreme acting situations where elements like grief, rage, and passion are pervasive. It is also important to avoid inappropriate pauses for breathing (especially when attempting to master long sentences) or breaking for emotional effect and distorting the meter from a mistaken sense of "poetic" presentation.

What is seen on the page should never be construed as a series of artfully crafted "pomes," but rather as a brilliant man of the theatre's careful and colorful word choices. Ben Jonson commented that Shakespeare "never blotted a line..." in his composition. This is strong evidence of his attention to word choices. Recent computer studies have affirmed that this particular playwright possessed a working vocabulary of some 25,000 words. This compares impressively to our average core of approximately 15,000. These diverse "word images" complement the needs of characters in specific circumstances. Such thoughtful choices require the support of strong performance technique in actors. Try to always remember that CHARACTERIZATION and the VERSE are INSEPARABLE. Verse will quickly transform from the obstacle the student actor may have feared to an invaluable aid to acting Shakespeare.

When confronting the challenges of acting in verse and employing such colorful and dynamic language, the performing artist must be BOLD. Using committed and "risk-filled" strokes on the broad canvas mentioned earlier, the actor must be prepared to savor words in a uniquely enthusiastic manner. He must be willing to make unaccustomed emotional investment and expend energy in a way that goes beyond what may have been required in earlier situations. He must approach the work like an athlete, primed and at the ready. Shakespearean characters are seldom at rest — they are always in extremity calling for levels of expression best served by colorful language.

The actor must be prepared to create moments of struggle and portray great emotion. He must support that emotion by exploring vocal techniques that might call for variation in volume, wide pitch, and sustained vowel sounds, requiring an open mouth and placement of full value on internal and terminal consonants. Practice with vocal color will always produce good results, but never more than in Shakespeare. The student actor must never be afraid to do it wrong. There can be no "wrong" when exploration of this rich material is undertaken. In addition, the Shakespearean actor cannot be hesitant to punch the words that matter most ("operatives"). As vocal goals like these are realized, the actor discovers that his choices prove to be not only what the verse dictates, but also what his character requires. To repeat, the verse that Shakespeare wrote SUPPORTS characterization. Act the text! In Shakespeare the text and the subtext are the same thing. Just do it!

Another useful device in learning to work with verse is the knowledge and application of the technique called "scansion." Scansion is the actor's attention to the number of syllables and the stress called for in lines of poetry. (For example, iambic pentameter, Shakespeare's favored form, calls for ten syllables with alternating light and dark emphasis). As he "scans" Shakespearean text, the actor finds assistance in "hidden direction" (John Barton of the Royal Shakespeare Company coined this term), which provides many cues to aid him in his choices. Scansion, like improvisation or paraphrasing, can be a valuable rehearsal tool to assist in uncovering the nuances of line readings. (See Unit Six, Using Stress to Create Meaning.)

Finally, the actor preparing to do this work must commit to the sensual quality of Shakespeare's words. He must revel in them. Wallow in them! Enjoy new words—Shakespeare's actors and audiences did. Make everything uttered seem to come from the very heart of your being, arriving in the world of the play for the very first time. That sense of newly coined language is important for the spontaneity, dynamic, and color that make Shakespeare resonate over the generations. Use it. Many of the words the Elizabethans employed were coined in the moment and were part of the development of a youthful and energetic language. Enjoy displaying emotions and the words they evoke. Project yourself back in time to Elizabethan England and gain pleasure from thinking and talking as they might have. Once again, savor those words. Use them as living, breathing things with which to express yourself as an actor and as a human being. "The play's the thing." Under no circumstances let the actor take on more importance than the play. Permit the text to tell you what to do. Believe in it. Trust in it. DO it!

SUMMARY

1. Follow the punctuation, not the arrangement on the page.

2. Put SIMPLE COMMUNICATION first.

3. Just play your intentions. Support the "argument."

4. Make friends with the verse. Forget that much of it is poetry and think of it as the heightened language required for the extreme situations of the plays.

5. Acknowledge that the verse and the characters are inseparable.

6. Be BOLD!

7. Begin learning about "scansion."

8. Savor the words both in verse and in prose.

9. Trust the text.

Exercise One
THE MINILOGUE

The following "minilogues" will give the student actor an opportunity to experience acting in verse. Select one that you like and memorize it, incorporating the suggestions you have read in this unit.

The goal of the exercise is not to "know" the play thoroughly or to explore context, but rather to simply make sense of the language and to apply it boldly and with energy. GO FOR IT! Don't worry about right or wrong. It will be better to be outrageously wrong than right while "too close to the vest."

When performed, the minilogue should reward you with an exhilarating feeling of risk-taking and athleticism. If you fall short of this feeling, do it over until you have expended the same kind of energy that you might have in running a 100-yard dash

MINILOGUES

Hermia (MND):

    I do entreat your Grace to pardon me.
    I know not by what power I am made bold,
    Nor how it may concern my modesty,
    In such a presence here to plead my thoughts;
    But I beseech your Grace that I may know
    The worst that may befall me in this case,
    If I refuse to wed Demetrius.

Helena (MND):

    Can you not hate me, as I know you do,
    But you must join in souls to mock me too?
    If you were men, as men you are in show,
    You would not use a gentle lady so;
    To vow, and swear, and superpraise my parts,
    When I am sure you hate me with your hearts.
    You both are rivals, and love Hermia;
    And now both rivals, to mock Helena.

A trim exploit, a manly enterprise,
To conjure tears up in a poor maid's eyes
With your derision!

Helena (MND):

Call you me fair? That fair again unsay.
Demetrius loves your fair. O happy fair!
Your eyes are lodestars, and your tongue's sweet air
More tuneable than lark to shepherd's ear
When wheat is green, when hawthorn buds appear.
Sickness is catching. O, were favor so,
Yours would I catch, fair Hermia, ere I go!

Viola (TN):

I am no fee'd post, lady; keep your purse,
My master, not myself, lacks recompense.
Love make his heart of flint, that you shall love,
And let your fervor, like my master's, be
Placed in contempt! Fairwell, fair cruelty.

Viola (TN):

By innocence I swear, and by my youth
I have one heart, one bosom, and one truth,
And that no woman has, nor never none
Shall mistress be of it, save I alone.
And so adieu, good madam. Nevermore
Will I my master's tears to you deplore.

Lady Macbeth (*Macbeth*):

The raven himself is hoarse
That croaks the fatal entrance of Duncan
Under my battlements. Come, you spirits
That tend on mortal thoughts, unsex me here,
And fill me from the crown to the toe top-full
Of direst cruelty!

Olivia (TN):

Cesario, by the roses of the spring,
By maidenhood, honor, truth and every thing
I love thee so, that, maugre all thy pride,

Nor wit nor reason can my passion hide.
Do not extort thy reasons from this clause,
For that I woo, thou therefore hast no cause;
But rather reason thus with reason fetter,
Love sought is good, but given unsought is better

Ophelia (*Hamlet*):

O, what a noble mind is here o'erthrown!
The courtier's, soldier's, scholar's, eye, tongue,sword,
Th' expectation and rose of the fair state,
The glass of fashion and the mould of form,
Th' observ'd of all observers, quite, quite down!

Phoebe (AYLI):

He said mine eyes were black and my hair black,
And, now I am rememb'red, scorn'd at me.
I marvel why I answer'd not again.
But that's all one; omittance is no quittance.
I'll write to him a very taunting letter,
And thou shalt bear it; wilt thou, Silvius?

Claudius (*Hamlet*):

And let the kettle to the trumpet speak,
And trumpet to the cannoneer without,
The cannons to the heavens, the heaven to earth,
"Now the King drinks to Hamlet."

Othello (*Othello*):

I have done the state some service, and they know't;
No more of that.
I pray you, in your letters,
When you shall these unlucky deeds relate,
Speak of me as I am; nothing extenuate,
Nor set down aught in malice: then, must you speak
Of one that lov'd not wisely, but too well.

Macbeth (*Macbeth*):

> To-morrow, and to-morrow, and to-morrow,
> Creeps in this petty pace from day to day,
> To the last syllable of recorded time;
> And all our yesterdays have lighted fools
> The way to dusty death. Out, out, brief candle!
> Life's but a walking shadow, a poor player,
> That struts and frets his hour upon the stage,
> And then is heard no more. It is a tale
> Told by an idiot, full of sound and fury,
> Signifying nothing.

Hamlet (*Hamlet*):

> What a piece of work is man, how noble in reason,
> how infinite in faculty, in form and moving, how
> express and admirable in action, how like an angel in
> apprehension, how like a god! The beauty of the world;
> the paragon of animals; and yet, to me, what is this
> quintessence of dust? Man delights not me—nor women
> neither, though by your smiling you seem to say so.

Jaques (AYLI):

> All the world's a stage
> And all the men and women merely players;
> They have their exits and their entrances,
> And one man in his time plays many parts,
> His acts being seven ages.

Prospero (*The Tempest*):

> Our revels now are ended.These our actors,
> As I foretold you, were all spirits, and
> Are melted into air, into thin air;
> And, like the baseless fabric of this vision,
> The cloud-capp'd tow'rs, the gorgeous palaces,
> The solemn temples, the great globe itself,
> Yea, all which it inherit, shall dissolve,
> And, like this insubstantial pageant faded,
> Leave not rack behind. We are such stuff
> As dreams are made on; and our little life
> Is rounded with a sleep.

Malcolm (*Macbeth*):

     My liege,
     They are not yet come back. But I have spoke
     With one that saw him die; who did report
     That very frankly he confess'd his treasons,
     Implor'd your Highness' pardon, and set forth
     A deep repentance. Nothing in his life
     Became him like the leaving it.

Brutus (JC):

     There is a tide in the affairs of men
     Which, taken at the flood, leads on to fortune;
     Omitted, all the voyage of their life
     Is bound in shallows and in miseries.
     On such a full sea are we now afloat;
     And we must take the current when it serves,
     Or lose our ventures.

Unit Two

ARCHAIC LANGUAGE

Coming to Terms with Antiquated Words and Phrases

A man of fire-new words.
—Berowne in *Love's Labours Lost*

Many of the words and phrases that first appeared in Shakespeare are now commonplace. This may be evidenced in what Northwestern State University of Louisiana's "Shakesperience" Tour has come to call "The Patter." Based on a narrative called "Enthusiasms" by Bernard Levin, this colorful tapestry of words and phrases is presented in a spirited and contemporary fashion with alternating and humorous characterization. It is recommended as an exercise to demonstrate that language we use daily is rooted in Shakespeare. This chapter begins with an assignment using the familiar phrases of the "Patter."

"THE SHAKESPEARE PATTER"
(Do Exercise 2. at the end of this unit now.)

Unlike the readily recognized vocabulary of the "Patter," many words encountered in Shakespeare are archaic and no longer in use ("bare bodkins" and foul bombards" are seldom topics of conversation today). But to Shakespeare's audiences, the words (new or old) were ALL! Theatre patrons went to "hear a play," not to "see a play." They focused on the language of the performances in a manner that no longer exists. For us, communicating with antiquated language and utilizing references bound to other cultures present special actor problems and prove intimidating when encountered for the first time. But just as many words we use in the articles, stories, plays, and novels of the present will require some form of explanation to future readers, so research, glossaries, and footnotes must be relied upon to clarify meanings of words no longer in popular use for the contemporary Shakespearean artist. Don't treat this as overly problematic.

The first and probably most effective way to become comfortable with such words and phrases in Shakespeare is to READ and to read widely. Not only immersion in the plays themselves, but a vigorous campaign of reading anything that broadens vocabulary will strengthen the English language base necessary for working with Shakespeare. His vocabulary was powerful. One valuable exercise is to paraphrase antiquated material into contemporary English until its meanings become natural and may be said to be "your own." Affectations, like the employment of "appliqued" British accents, are NOT worth pursuing. They indicate a step toward stilted and limited communication. Good old Standard American English possesses both the clarity and the energy needed to support any Shakespearean role. The last thing needed for a successful "Shakesperience" is pretension.

In rehearsal or during the preparation period for classroom presentation, it often proves useful to permit a looser rein for interpretive gesture, inflection, facial expression, and bearing in attempts to communicate. The words must carry the audience along in the required or desired direction, but these actor skills can provide needed reinforcement.

Since specific archaic words, phrases, and forms prove relatively consistent in the plays, as time passes, there will be less and less need to "dig" for meanings of obscure words or to research references bound to bygone cultures. They are systematically added to your working actor's vocabulary by a literary osmosis. You just pick them up.

Another important factor to consider is the significance of Elizabethan stage conventions. There were certain stage techniques that were common to the theatre of the time. For example, treating the audience somewhat "presentationally" (acknowledging their presence in the acting space as a kind of ideal "confidante") was common practice. This knowledge allows you to boldly break the "Fourth Wall" of naturalistic theatre practice at appropriate times and mix the intimate with the more spectacular.

Archaic language sometimes requires the student actor to turn to emphasis, or even word or phrase substitution to solve communication problems with contemporary audiences. Decisions as to whether "'tis nobler in the mind" to carry a modern audience backward in time or to find ways to bring the play forward will prove the center of many actor-director discussions now and in the future. (See Unit Fourteen. The Matrix.) Although subjective, compromises in these areas may make the difference between successfully contacting an audience and falling victim to the "museum" qualities associated with classical literature. Above all, you must create the same kind of "world" or reality with Shakespeare's material as that you bring to the most accessible plays in your repertory. By keeping readings specific and fresh, the performer makes the audience listen and carries them along through the sometimes unfamiliar word order, using every available actor's device to make the antiquated word or convention credible and comprehensible. Many of the words the Elizabethans used in these plays were also brand new to them. Their language was growing, and the coining of words was a common practice, even among ordinary tradesmen and peasants. This is one reason why actors around the world often support the view that American English, with its youthful dynamic and rougher, less genteel energy, is closer to what Elizabethan audiences would have experienced at their theatres than is the more proper British articulation of the Shakespearean text.

Beyond the use of the second person "thee" and "thou" (forms that were on their way out of common usage by 1600) and the vocabulary itself, archaic language can also be elusive in the way contractions are structured and combined. Familiarity with these forms will aid the beginning student-actor tremendously in the understanding of much of the antiquated syntax in the plays.

"Will" was regularly shortened to "'ll" (as in I'll and he'll). However, the Elizabethan apparently chose not to use "n't" for "not" (as in contemporary won't, can't, don't, shouldn't). Apart from the exclusion of these "not" forms, the following are some selected examples of the way contractions not in common usage in the modern world were used in Shakespeare's day.

Apostrophe "t":

't was used for "it" at the beginning of a verb (as in 'twill, 'tis)

't was used also for "it" at the end of a verb (as in know't, show't, be't, swear't, is't)

't for "it" at the end of a preposition (as in for't, on't, to't)

't for "to" at the beginning of a verb that begins with a vowel

(as in t'express, t'observe, t'undo)

"Th" and "I" (as in th' for "the" (th'answer)

and "I'" for "in" (i'time, i'th' earth)

The practice of shortening individual words to fewer than the standard number of syllables was commonplace (allowing, among other things, for a more flexible use of beats in a line of poetry).
For example:

"heav'n" for heaven, "dev'l" for devil, "ev'l" for evil, "pow'r" for power,

"spir't" for spirit, "fun'ral" for funeral and "be'ng" for being.

Other forms often encountered are:

" 'gainst" for against

"ta'en" for taken

"a'" for "at" or for "he"

" 'er" as in "e'er" for ever; "o'er" for over

" 'st" for "est" as in "think'st" or "look'st"

"op'd" for opened

" 'n" for "en" as in "fall'n" for fallen

" 'r" for "er" as in "flow'r" for flower, "show'r" for shower

"desp'rate" for desperate or "temp'ring" for tempering

" 's" for "es" as in " 'scape" for escape, " 'stablish" for establish

These antiquated forms are also used with frequency, and, once the student actor has become familiar with how they function, they are no obstacle to comprehension. Of course, some obsolete words will simply need to be looked up and incorporated into the actor's classical vocabulary and rehearsal routine. Do not be intimidated. Do not make the common mistake of thinking that others already know all these things and have possessed this vocabulary since birth. Everyone needs to learn Shakespeare IN PROCESS. On-the-job training produces good results.

SUMMARY

1. Become familiar with words and phrases minted in Shakespeare's time.

2. Don't be put off by the archaic. Welcome research, glossaries, and footnotes.

3. READ! (The Shakespeare plays and all good literature.)

4. Paraphrase the material to assist in making it your own.

5. Avoid affectation (especially phony British).

6. Use acting tools like inflection, gesture, and facial expression to help communicate archaic syntax.

7. Become familiar with Elizabethan stage conventions.

8. Study the contractions, ellipses, and other forms provided in this chapter.

EXERCISE 2
THE SHAKESPEARE PATTER

The goal of this exercise is to increase the actor's appreciation of just how much of the English language first found expression in the words of William Shakespeare. Once again, working with small bits of material, the students will experience identifying and attacking operative words with the bold vocality called for in the plays.

The "Patter" should be performed by groups of six. Actors should be encouraged to add to the "snowball" (cumulative) effect of the piece by savoring each new contribution even more than his predecessor. Actors – MOVE! and look for acting teacher Michael Shurtleff's "love" and "humor" in the process. (For example, make property "vanish," DON'T "budge an inch," BE "tongue-tied," DANCE "attendance on your lord and master," BE an "eyesore," or a "blinking idiot"). It should be impossible to go too far. Take your risks and have fun. In fact, risk-taking and boldness should be the only goal of this exercise.

(As Arranged and Performed by the "Shakesperience" Tour Group of Northwestern State University, Louisiana.)

(In this particular presentation, Actors A, B and F were males; C, D and E were females.)

Actor A. If you cannot understand my argument and declare

Actor B. "It's Greek to me!"

Actor A. You are quoting Shakespeare.

Actor C. If you claim to be more sinned against than sinning,

Actor A. You are quoting Shakespeare.

Actor D. If you recall your salad days, you are quoting Shakespeare;

Actor E. If you act more in sorrow than in anger,

Actor F. If your wish is father to the thought,

Actor C. If your lost property has vanished into thin air,

Actor A. You are quoting Shakespeare.

Actor A. If you have ever refused to budge an inch

Actors C and E. or suffered from green-eyed jealousy,

Actor D. If you have played fast and loose,

Actor F. If you have been tongue-tied,

Actor B. A tower of strength,

Actor C. hoodwinked,

Actor A. or in a pickle;

Actor E. If you have knitted your brows,

Actor A. Made a virtue of necessity,

Men.   Insisted on fair play

Actor B. Slept not one wink,

Actor C. Stood on ceremony,

Women.   Danced attendance (on your lord and master),

Actor D. Laughed yourself into stitches,

Actor E.   had short shrift,

Actor B.   cold comfort,

Actor A.   or too much of a good thing,

Actors C and D.   If you have seen better days

Actor F.   or lived in a Fool's Paradise

Actor A.   Why, be that as it may,

Actor D.   (The more fool you)

Actor A.   For it is a foregone conclusion that you are

Actor E.   (As good luck would have it)

All.   Quoting Shakespeare!

Actor C.   If you clear out bag and baggage,

Actor E.   If you think it is high time,

Actor C.   and that that is the long

Actor D.   and short

Both C and D. of it,

Actor B.   If you believe the game is up

Actor F.   and the truth will out,

Actor A.   even if it involves your own flesh and blood—

Actor D.   If you lie low

Actor B.   'Til the crack of doom

Actor C.   because you suspect foul play —

Actor F.   If you have your teeth set on edge,

Actors D and E. at one fell swoop,

Actor C.   without rhyme or reason;

Actor E.   Then, to give the Devil his due

Actor A.   If the truth were known

Actor D.   (For surely you have a tongue in your head)

All.   You are quoting Shakespeare!

Actor C. Even if you bid me good riddance and send me packing

Actor F. If you wish I was dead as a door nail,

Actor B. If you think I am an eyesore,

Actor A. a laughing stock,

Actor C. the Devil incarnate,

Actor E. a stony-hearted villain,

Actor D. bloody-minded,

Actor F. or a blinking idiot —

Actor C. Then, by Jove,

Actor D. Oh, Lord,

Actor A. Tut, tut,

Actor E. For goodness' sake,

Actor F. What the dickens

All.   But me no but's,

Actor B. It is all one to me—

All.   For you are quoting Shakespeare!

           —Based on Bernard Levin's "Enthusiasms," 1983

Unit Three

PAINTING ON A BROADER CANVAS

Rising to the Epic Demands of Shakespearean Performance

Boldness be my friend.

Iachimo in *Cymbeline*

Shakespeare's characters are typically portrayed at their brightest and most intense (appearing at the height of rage, in the depths of despair, or suffering the pangs of unrequited love). Characters in modern plays (no matter how psychologically engaging they may be) lack the size that is called for in Shakespearean performance. The latter roles are written at a bolder level and are painted with broad strokes on a large canvas. Certainly other playwrights have attained mastery of the theatrical miniature, the portrait, and even the landscape; but only the work of Shakespeare should be approached like a massive mural.

The characters are heroic and archetypal, ranging from rude mechanicals to monarchs. Rising to the demands of "lunatics, lovers, and poets" enmeshed in such intense situations requires the actor to put aside the looser and more lethargic manner of his customary theatre practice and be prepared to provide the muscular, controlled physicality demanded by the size of these plays. He often addresses language that inherently denotes rank, education and intelligence of high-born characters, and must perform with the grace, carriage, and eloquence of gesture required to support credible portrayal.

The Shakespearean actor is required not only to present a graceful and articulate (the Elizabethans were a "verbal" culture) presence onstage but also to become practiced in the use of period weapons and in diverse dance movement (from the gavotte to the Morris dance). Since the locales of the plays are often exotic, he must learn to move easily in costumes representing many eras, from flowing gowns with impossible sleeves to full battle armor. He must strive to avoid small, close gestures in favor of the broader and more expansive physical actions that are called for in epic plays. As suggested in Unit One, the actor must commit to greater effort vocally, always articulating carefully, giving full and energetic attention to vowel sounds, opening his mouth, providing breath support like a trained singer, and giving full value to all internal as well as terminal consonants.

This unit has supported the concept that characters, the "personae" of Shakespeare's plays (and the actors portraying them) NEED the language they employ in order to support their reactions to the intense circumstances in which the playwright has placed them. Other words would not suffice. Just as in a modern musical comedy, a song emerges when the message is too big for dialogue alone, so the moment of the soliloquy or the confrontation in Shakespeare demands urgency. Bearing in mind that the Elizabethans loved conversation and that the characters on their stages valued skill with speech as they did ability with weapons and wooing practices, it is clear that public display of emotion was an accepted, even desired practice. This high emotional level is what colors the broad canvas. The unembarrassed display of intense emotion is at the core of playing Shakespeare effectively and should be welcomed by the student actor. Notice that Shakespeare's characters consistently speak truthfully and wear their hearts on their sleeves, or if not, they use soliloquies or asides to share secret thoughts. The ability to pour your heart out in a soliloquy must become a part of your actor-arsenal and is a necessary part of acting in the epic play.

Here is a chance to cut loose!

UNEMBARRASSED EMOTION

(Do Exercise 3. at the end of this unit.)

It must be noted that the skilled actor must not only strive to understand the complexity of the emotions in his character, but to DISPLAY in his acting a desire to make sense of them. This is where interesting conflict is revealed. You cannot play an emotion. Master acting teacher Uta Hagen once said, "Mood is Doom spelled backwards," and the Royal Shakespeare Company's John Barton assures actors that there is no such thing as a "sad" speech, suggesting (with Hagen) that all emotive efforts must be specific and immediate to the circumstances of the play. Shakespeare's personae live, act and react in the eternal present tense, the "here and now." The Shakespearean actor's emotional investment must be large enough to demand the words he is provided because he will be unable to get what he WANTS (his objective, intention) without them. As a performing artist, he is then called upon to creatively MIX moments in which he allows emotion to predominate with others where he allows his character's intellectual capacity to stand apart and "handle" those emotions.

No matter how fraught with consequence the epic demands of the play may be or how much the actor raises the stakes, the surface sense is always there. Find that sense first. From there, explore what will bring you to a bold and moving portrayal. This will take some time. Don't expect full-blown characterizations too soon.

The "size" of Shakespearean portrayal is compounded by the fact that many scenes come at spectacular moments in the lives of the characters — weddings, rituals, and other public events evoking pomp and grandeur. Once again, the need for bold, graceful strokes and epic portrayal is asserted. Follow Shakespeare's own advice as he penned it in his famous "Advice to the Players" in *Hamlet*.

> Hamlet: Speak the speech, I pray you, as I pronounc'd it to you, trippingly on the tongue, but if you mouth it, as many of our players do, I had as lief the town-crier spoke my lines. Nor do not saw the air too much with your hand, thus, but use all gently, for in the very torrent, tempest, and, as I may say, whirlwind of your passion, you must acquire and beget a temperance that may give it smoothness. O, it offends me to the soul to hear a robustious periwig-pated fellow tear a passion to tatters, to very rags, to split the ears of the groundlings,

who, for the most part, are capable of nothing

but inexplicable dumb shows and noise. I would

have such a fellow whipt for o'erdoing Termagant, it

out-Herods Herod, pray you avoid it. ……

Be not too tame neither, but let your own

discretion be your tutor. Suit the action to the word,

the word to the action, with this special observance,

that you o'erstep not the modesty of nature: for any

thing so o'erdone is from the purpose of playing,

whose end, both at the first and now, was and is, to

hold as 'twere the mirror up to nature: to show virtue

her own feature, scorn her own image, and the very age and

body of the time his form and pressure. Now this overdone,

or come tardy off, though it makes the un-

skillful laugh, cannot but make the judicious grieve; the

censure of which one must in your allowance o'erweigh

a whole theatre of others. O, there be players

that I have seen play – and heard others praise, and

that highly —- not to speak it profanely, that,

neither having th' accent of Christians nor the gait of

Christian, pagan, nor man, have so strutted and

bellow'd that I have thought some of Nature's journeymen

had made men, and not made them well, they

imitated humanity so abominably.

And let those that play the clowns speak no more than
    is set down for them,

for there be of them that will themselves

laugh to set on some quantity of barren spectators to laugh too, though in the mean time some necessary question of the play be then to be consider'd. That's villainous, and shows a most pitiful ambition in the fool that uses it.

SUMMARY:

1. Shakespeare's characters are found at their most intense.

2. This intensity calls for increased size and bold strokes.

3. Attention must be paid to rank (many of Shakespeare's characters are high-born and privileged).

4. Familiarity with weapons and period movement is important.

5. Reassert boldness in language.

6. An unembarrassed display of emotion is required.

7. Follow Shakespeare's own advice.

EXERCISE 3
UNEMBARRASSED EMOTION

Below are two monologues (one for men and one for women). Work on these monologues, pulling all stops. Tear your hair, beat your breast, roll on the floor, whatever it takes to make your instructor feel the need to "pull you back." The goal here is to go TOO FAR. Once you have achieved a kind of complete abandon to the material and have been judged willing to put it "on the line," then work the speech in the same manner as any other acting exercise with the understanding that you have first explored the most extreme and intense levels of the piece.

MEN

Romeo (R and J): (He is in tears and nearly mad with grief.)

Tis torture, and not mercy. Heaven is here,

Where Juliet lives, and every cat and dog

And little mouse, every unworthy thing,

Live here in heaven, and may look on her,

But Romeo may not. More validity,

More honorable state, more courtship lives

In carrion flies than Romeo; they may seize

On the white wonder of dear Juliet's hand,

And steal immortal blessing from her lips,

Who, even in pure and vestal modesty,

Still blush, as thinking their own kisses sin;

But Romeo may not, he is banished.

This may flies do, when I from this must fly;

They are free men, but I am banished:

And sayest thou yet that exile is not death?

Hadst thou no poison mix'd, no sharp-ground knife,

No sudden mean of death, though ne'er so mean,

But "banished" to kill me? "Banished"?

O, friar, the damned use that word in hell;

Howling attends it. How hast thou the heart,

Being a divine, a ghostly confessor,

A sin-absolver, and my friend profess'd,

To mangle me with that word "banished"?

WOMEN

Isabella (*Measure for Measure*): (Her brother has just asked her to give up her virginity to a powerful man in order to save his own life.)

> O you beast!
>
> O faithless coward! O, dishonest wretch!
>
> Wilt thou be made a man out of my vice?
>
> Is't not a kind of incest, to take life
>
> From thine own sister's shame? What should I think?
>
> Heaven shield my mother play'd my father fair!
>
> For such a warped slip of wilderness
>
> Ne'er issu'd from his blood. Take my defiance!
>
> Die, perish!   Might but my bending down
>
> Reprieve thee from thy fate, it should proceed.
>
> I'll pray a thousand prayers for thy death,
>
> No word to save thee.
>
> Mercy to thee would prove itself a bawd;
>
> 'Tis best that thou diest quickly.

Unit Four
RHYME, BLANK VERSE OR PROSE?
Painting with Light and Shadow

"The poet's eye, in a fine frenzy rolling, doth glance from heaven to earth, from earth to heaven, and as imagination bodies forth the forms of things unknown, the poet's pen turns them to shapes and gives to airy nothing a local habitation and a name."

Theseus in *A Midsummer Night's Dream*

Brutus (Julius Caesar): Be patient to the last.

Romans, countrymen, and lovers, hear me for my cause,

And be silent, that you may hear. Believe me for mine

Honor, and have respect to mine honor, that you

May believe. Censure me in your wisdom, and awake

Your senses, that you may the better judge. If there

Be any in this assembly, any dear friend of Caesar's, to

Him I say, that Brutus' love to Caesar was no less than

His. If then that friend demand why Brutus rose

Against Caesar, this is my answer: Not that I lov'd

Caesar less, but that I lov'd Rome more.

Brutus' words are the beginning of one of the most often quoted speeches in all Shakespearean canon. Yet, it is not written in verse. So far, our emphasis has been on poetry since this is the form that most beginners associate with Shakespearean acting. But, in truth, almost thirty percent of the content of the plays is in beautiful prose similar to Brutus' funeral oration. The non-prose is composed of either blank verse or rhymed poetry carefully chosen by the playwright in appropriate proportion to produce the best possible dramatic effect.

(For example, *The Merry Wives of Windsor* is nearly ninety percent prose supporting the rank, or lack of rank, of the characters in the play; *Julius Caesar* and *Richard III* are each over ninety percent blank verse since neither the prosaic nor the lofty sentiments of rhymed poetry serve the needs of the historical figures in such events; and plays like *A Midsummer Night's Dream* and *Love's Labours Lost* rank high — nearly fifty percent— in rhymed poetic content, this time providing support to the sentimental natures of the dramatis personae). The point is that Shakespeare is not composed of only the "pomes" that neophyte acting students fear they will encounter when venturing into the world of the man from Stratford.

As student actors you should know that prose (at least prose as Shakespeare created it) is no less intense, dynamic, or colorful than its verse counterpart. Having learned earlier that the plays may be approached as "heightened language" and not poetic outpourings, you soon realize that actors must treat prose content in the same manner as poetry. Your performance responsibility is to bring it to life, whether presented on the page in prose or in verse. Leave the study of the structural differences to the scholars. Just believe firmly in what your character says and does and proceed from there. Similar artistic techniques and utilization of emotional resources should be brought to the speeches, whatever their form. When Shakespeare chooses to use prose, it is certain that there is a dramatic reason for it, beyond variety, that will serve to enrich the actor.

It has been suggested that the prose-verse distinction simply differentiates between the upper and lower classes. This is an oversimplification. Just as Shakespeare allowed Brutus to speak in prose in order to argue on the level of the common people he was seeking to sway AND as he later couches Marc Antony's soaring response in verse to affect the mob in a different manner, so he uses a skillful balance of poetry and prose to gain multiple objectives besides simple class or caste identification. It is true he does often illuminate levels in society by the speech patterns they use; but he also cleverly achieves many other emotional goals by switching from one mode to another in order to arrive at dramatic effect or emphasis. In fact, the actor may consider alternation between verse and prose as a stage direction of a sort and use it to assist his interpretation.

On occasion, the playwright deliberately marries naturalistic or common conversation with heightened speech for a change in direction, allowing reality to break in on romance or highlighting an attempt at logic. Other times the use of prose for logic and verse for emotion IS his creative device. Elsewhere he simply achieves "levels" among his characters through the forms by which they express themselves.

Are there occasions when one or the other is more "likely" to be used? Here are some helpful generalizations. The actor will find verse spoken in most ceremonies and rituals, including coronations, weddings, and funerals. Elders tend to speak in verse (unless they are rustics or broad comic characters). It is common to find high-ranking officers and courtiers employing verse. Those in the throes of love and those grappling with extremely "heavy" thoughts also resort to verse for adequate expression. Verse is employed when key plot points are emphasized, at turning points, and when new or significant characters enter or leave the stage.

Prose, in contrast, for those "not born under a rhyming planet," will be found in rustic characters, fools, and others who are earthy or bawdy by nature. The prosaic is also found in casual meetings and inevitably in gossip sessions. Whenever scenes involving freewheeling, easy-going characters are encountered or when situations involving basic instincts are depicted, you are apt to find prose as the chosen literary device.

There are no set rules for the use of verse over ordinary prose. But, when you see prose used, be assured that you will discover the same kind of solid literary and dramatic rationale undergirding it as when verse is the choice (as illustrated by the mob psychology exhibited by both Brutus and Marc Antony in their funeral speeches). Examining a few more lines of the famous oration by Brutus demonstrates the "poetic" power that can be contained in Shakespeare's prose lines.

BRUTUS: Had you rather Caesar were living,

And die all slaves, than that Caesar were dead,

To live all free men? As Caesar lov'd me,

I weep for him; as he was fortunate, I rejoice

At it; as he was valiant, I honor him;

But, as he was ambitious, I slew him.

There is tears for his love;

Joy for his fortune; honor for his valor;

And death for his ambition. Who is here so base

That would be a bondman?

If any, speak, for him have I offended.

Who is here so rude that would not be a Roman?

If any, speak, for him have I offended.

Who is here so vile that will not love his country?

If any, speak, for him have I offended.

I pause for a reply.

Now, compare this to a rhymed poetic selection from a different play. Read both aloud:

CHORUS (R and J):

Now old desire doth in his death-bed lie,

And young affection gapes to be his heir;

That fair for which love groan'd for and would die,

With tender Juliet match'd is now not fair.

Now Romeo is belov'd and loves again,

Alike bewitched by the charm of looks;

But to his foe suppos'd he must complain,

And she steal love's sweet bait from fearful hooks.

Being held a foe, he may not have access

To breathe such vows as lovers use to swear,

And she as much in love, her means much less

To meet her new-beloved any where.

But passion lends them power, time means, to meet,

Temp'ring extremities with extreme sweet.

Your reading of these two speeches should make it clear that in terms of intensity and vocal color, one is equal to the other. Only the playwright's intent (just as actor's CHOICES determine objectives) dictates when he opts for prose and when for poetry. He strives for effect. Actors should simply commit to the same intensity for all forms, raising the stakes only when the needs of the character call for it. The more Shakespeare you read, the more you will find an ability to trust the playwright's choice of syntax, vocabulary, and form.

SUMMARY:

1. Shakespearean prose and verse are equally dynamic and colorful. (Since nearly thirty percent of the plays are prose, the author must have valued its potential.)

2. Both kinds of verse (rhymed and blank) are employed by the playwright for many reasons other than just class distinction.

3. Among these reasons are changes in emotional tone; achievement of levels; emphasis on logic over emotion giving full sway to the emotional; hitting key points; distinguishing among monarchs, courtiers, fools, lovers, madmen, bumpkins, gossips, and dozens of other character types.

4. Again, TRUST and use what the playwright gives you.

EXERCISE 4.
Using Either Verse or Prose to Motivate Audiences

Using the two selections provided earler in this unit, READ to one another. Make the prose from JULIUS CAESAR as expansive and colorful (poetic) as you can and the verse from ROMEO AND JULIET as naturalistic as possible. Then, reverse the process. You will find that either selection will support whatever emotional investment you may infuse into it. Remember, MAKE CHOICES and TAKE RISKS!

Unit Five

ANTITHESES AND OTHER PARALLELISMS
Using "Paired" Opposites Effectively

Set the word itself against the words.

-Richard II

Setting one word against another and using opposites are common literary devices. They are particularly effective in dramatic literature when the impact of the actor's inflection and other vocal and physical techniques help establish the preferred paired word.

Disguise fair nature with hard-favored rage.

—Henry V

This fragment from Henry's exhortation of his troops contrasts the nouns, "nature" and "rage" as well as their descriptive adjectives, "fair" and "hard-favored." It is an example of Shakespeare's use of parallel constructions. It also provides an illustration of antithesis.

Shakespeare thought in terms of duality. He did this with his characters and in the way he had them express themselves. Philosophically and psychologically, he acknowledged the dual nature of man, allowing for a "this BUT that" area of contradiction within the same human beings.

Antithesis, a favorite literary device with Shakespeare, establishes opposites that ask the reader/audience to accept a "not this, but that" choice. The structure informs us of what IS over what IS NOT selected for special significance and dramatic clout. Elizabethan playwriting conventions provide frequent examples of antithesis,and many of Shakespeare's peers enjoyed using the form. By supplying alternatives and playing them against one another, the playwright could evoke powerful comparisons and create magnificent imagery. Such opposites and contrasts provided rich diversity (especially for a society so in tune with stretching its linguistic muscles) and allowed scope for actors to employ stress or emphasis effectively.

But stress (emphasis, inflection) is not the only way to give paired words their desired value or meaning. Variation in volume, unexpected changes in articulation, elongation of vowel sounds, tapping chosen words, even the tone of voice can affect the balance and the subsequent impact of parallel words or phrases. Shakespeare apparently expected careful attention to this kind of work from members of his company, often leaving choices and decisions open to the actor's instincts. He deliberately leaves space for the performing artist to finish the work. Small wonder that Shakespeare is such a favorite of serious actors everywhere. To him, the actor was not a puppet or an instrument, but a colleague in bringing art to life. In addition, physical devices like body language, facial expression, and gesture can support choices combining the playwright's implied direction and the actor's decisions in playing the passages.

The parallel words or phrases need not be opposites. They might be contrasting images, sometimes paradoxical, even contradictory. By "home-working" paired words, the student-actor increases his understanding of the text and the literary conventions which fostered them. Comprehending these devices is extremely important since often it is antithesis that provides the "change in direction" in a passage, leaving the actor to "shift gears" in his preparation (rehearsal) and performance.

Inflection within the parallel structure serves to inform the audience. It invites them to join you in going where you want them to go. With the hundreds of examples of parallelisms in Shakespeare, familiarity with ways to support such constructions becomes a tremendous communication and acting tool. You must punch paired words differently as they provide operative forces in the passages, clarifying your choices as you commit to preferences. Returning to the *Henry V* example at the beginning of this chapter – is "nature" or "rage" the noun you opt to go to bat with? Is "fair" or "hard favor'd" the preferred member of the pair?

BRAKING. The temptation will exist to slow down for individual words or puns as you make decisions about emphasis. Be careful of this practice. That hesitation or stop may force you or your audience to derail and lose track of antecedents. Remember, some of these sentences are quite long. It is your responsibility to guide the audience. If

Shakespeare was written to play rapidly (it may well have been only "two-hour's traffic" on Elizabethan stages,taking into account overlapping cues and energetic, rapid-fire delivery), then you must pick up all cues. A practical way to approach a Shakespearean monologue (or even a play) is to begin line readings at a rate and pace slightly slower than what you arrive at several minutes into the work. Contemporary audiences may need a little getting-used-to-it time since, unlike in life, there will be no time to repeat it.

Another of Shakespeare's preferred devices is the oxymoron. This literary technique allows for back-to-back word contrast, usually a noun with a contradictory adjective. An example is Juliet's calling Romeo a "fiend-angelical." Obviously he cannot be a fiend and an angel at once, but her frustration makes the use of the mixed form wonderfully descriptive of her dilemma.

Before leaving this unit, let us look for just a moment at the importance of antecedents. Antecedents are, simply put, the words or ideas that went before. The actor must never let go of earlier significant words, phrases, or ideas since Shakespearean passages are often convoluted. Sonnet 29 provides an excellent exercise passage in which to consider the significance of the antecedent. The entire piece is composed of one sentence. There is no terminal punctuation until the end.

SUMMARY:

1. The use of "paired opposites" is a preferred Shakespearean device.
2. Antithesis is a major example of this.
3. Punching operative words in the pairs may affect rate.
4. The oxymoron and careful attention to antecedents are frequently used devices.

EXERCISE 5
ANTITHESIS

The following are four classic examples of antithesis. Work these with a partner. Take sides. One be the preferred alternative and the other play the secondary emphasis. But don't be satisfied with your first readings. After working the phrase, reverse roles.

Disguise fair nature

    With hard-favored rage.

... look like th' innocent flower,

    but be the serpent under't.

Asses are made to bear and so are you,

    women are made to bear, and so are you.

I come to bury Caesar,

    Not to praise him.

EXERCISE 6
THE OXYMORON

Identify the oxymorons in the following passage. Then run the selection, striving for full value in the paired words.

Juliet: O serpent heart, hid with a flow'ring face!

        Did ever dragon keep so fair a cave?

        Beautiful tyrant! Fiend angelical!

        Dove-feather'd raven! Wolvish-ravening lamb!

        Despised substance of divinest show!

Just opposite of what thou justly seem'st,

A damned saint, an honorable villain!

EXERCISE 7
ANTECEDENTS

Read the following sonnet aloud. First, make a strong commitment to a breathing pattern. Then, work it again with your major goal becoming a desire to keep your audience fully aware of what has gone before. See how well you can carry them along.

Sonnet 29.

When in disgrace with Fortune and men's eyes

I all alone beweep my outcast state,

And trouble deaf Heaven with my bootless cries,

And look upon myself and curse my fate,

Wishing me like to one more rich in hope,

Featur'd like him, like him with friends possess'd,

Desiring this man's art, and that man's scope,

With what I most enjoy contented least;

Yet in these thoughts myself almost despising,

Haply I think on thee, and then my state

(Like to the lark at break of day arising

From sullen earth) sings hymns at Heaven's gate,

For thy sweet love remember'd such wealth brings,

That then I scorn to change my state with kings.

Unit Six

SCANSION
Using Stress to Create Meaning

The true concord of well-tuned sounds.

—Sonnet 8

Now is an appropriate time to introduce "scansion." Scansion is the analysis of the rhythmic structure of verse. Lines of verse are marked into "feet," the basic unit of poetry. Using "da-dah," a line of verse may be divided into "iambs" or two-syllable units. In Shakespeare, the iamb's second syllable is stressed more than the first, giving it a "da-DAH" sound. "Iambic PENTameter" tells us that there are FIVE feet of "da-DAH" iambs, reading: "da-DAH, da-DAH, da-DAH, da-DAH, da-DAH," (that is, stressing beats 2-4-6-8-10). This iambic pentameter form is basic to Shakespeare and is the heartbeat of the verse sections of all the plays. By "scanning" a line of poetry to analyze meter, the student-actor can find needed assistance in determining how to stress, emphasize, articulate or punch syllables, words and phrases.

Stress serves to create meaning. Missing placement of emphasis or beating the meter unmercifully can create problems for the actor. Becoming comfortable with scansion should (like your greater facility with the verse itself) be a major asset to your comprehension and performance.

Volume is the easiest way to provide stress on a syllable, but variety in articulation and other actor's techniques for "coloring" language can be employed to bring about effective readings. It is important to understand that scansion, like improvisation or theatre games, is not to be treated as some kind of "enlightened path" to communication. It is simply a tool, albeit a very useful tool, which will produce immediate and unexpected results.

As with the rhymed verse, iambic pentameter is the core of Shakespeare's blank verse. In fact, blank verse IS unrhymed iambic pentameter. Whenever the actor performs in verse, he should always explore the potential of expanding, modifying, compressing, or contracting beats to make the scansion regular. It is interesting to realize that you will find the more consideration you give to the possibilities of the meter, the more agreement emerges with what the author had in mind for the character.

You will also discover that Shakespeare takes liberties with strict adherence to any form. He does this in his application of meter. If he ends a line with the stressed syllable, that line is said to be "masculine." If there is an eleventh syllable, unstressed, the line is said to have a "feminine ending." This was not uncommon practice, but the art with which this playwright conjures with it is impressive.

A phrase such as "To BE or NOT to BE, that IS the QUES....tion." illustrates the use of the feminine ending. Actors may choose to question Shakespeare's reasons for doing this, but be assured, that after some research, you will find not only a satisfactory reason, but some insights which will aid your reading of the line. Try this right now. See if you can determine why this famous introductory line has a feminine ending.

Let us examine some rhymed poetry and some bits of blank verse to practice scanning for stress, all the while seeking clues to more dynamic and beautiful reading as well as the character implications that might come to mind.

Rhymed Poetry:

Helena (MND):

> How happy some o'er other some can be!
>
> Through Athens I am thought as fair as she.
>
> But what of that? Demetrius thinks not so;
>
> He will not know what all but he do know;
>
> And as he errs, doting on Hermia's eyes,
>
> So I, admiring of his qualities.
>
> Things base and vile, holding no quantity,

Love can transpose to form and dignity.

Love looks not with the eyes but with the mind;

And therefore is wing'd Cupid painted blind.

Nor hath Love's mind of any judgement taste;

Wings, and no eyes, figure unheedy haste;

And therefore is Love said to be a child,

Because in choice he is so oft beguiled.

As waggish boys in game themselves forswear,

So the boy Love is perjur'd every where;

For ere Demetrius look'd on Hermia's eyne,

He hail'd down oaths that he was only mine;

And when this hail some heat from Hermia felt,

So he dissolv'd, and show'rs of oaths did melt.

Blank Verse.

Anne (*Richard III*):

Blush, blush, thou lump of foul deformity;

For 'tis thy presence that exhales this blood

From cold and empty veins where no blood dwells.

Thy deed inhuman and unnatural

Provokes this deluge most unnatural.

O God! Which his blood mad'st, revenge his death!

O earth! Which this blood drinks't, revenge his death!

Either heav'n with lightning strike the murth'rer dead;

Or earth gape open wide and eat him quick,

As thou dost swallow up this good king's blood,

Which this hell-govern'd arm hath butchered!

OR

Richard (*Richard III*):

> Teach not thy lips such scorn; for they were   made
>
> For kissing, lady, not for such contempt.
>
> If thy revengeful heart cannot forgive,
>
> Lo, here I lend thee this sharp-pointed sword,
>
> Which if thou please to hide in this true breast,
>
> And let the soul forth that adoreth thee,
>
> I lay it naked to the deadly stroke,
>
> And humbly beg the death upon my knee.

Another device that Shakespeare enjoyed was SHARING poetic lines. In the next example, Romeo and Juliet alternate in rhymed verse. It is also interesting to note that this scene, if removed from the play's context, is a complete 14-line shared sonnet. Sonnets will be addressed in Unit Eleven as a separate acting experience.

Romeo and Juliet:

Romeo:

> If I profane with my unworthiest hand
>
> This holy shrine, the gentle fine is this,
>
> My lips, two blushing pilgrims, ready stand
>
> To smooth that rough touch with a tender kiss.

Juliet:

> Good pilgrim, you do wrong your hand too 'much,
>
> Which mannerly devotion shows in this:
>
> For saints have hands that pilgrims' hands do touch,

And palm to palm is holy palmers' kiss.

Romeo: Have not saints lips, and holy palmers too?

Juliet: Ay, pilgrim, lips that they must use in pray'r.

Romeo: O then, dear saint, let lips do what hands do,

They pray; grant thou, lest faith turn to despair.

Juliet: Saints do not move, though grant for prayer's sake.

Romeo: Then move not while my prayer's effect I take.

SUMMARY:

1. Learning to "scan" lines will create a useful tool for interpreting Shakespeare properly.

2. The ability to identify iambic pentameter and other verse forms expands your actor's arsenal.

3. It is valuable to know the difference between rhymed verse and blank verse.

4. There are sometimes feminine endings to lines of verse which permit additional beats.

5. Shakespeare permits characters to share verse.

EXERCISE 8

Using the examples in this unit, become as familiar with the process of scansion as possible. Be certain that you understand that this tool can be used as readily with blank verse as with rhymed poetry. Try using it on both. Immerse yourself in it since you "learn Shakespeare by doing Shakespeare."

A MACBETH Montage.
Northwestern State University, Louisiana

A wide range of character " types."
AS YOU LIKE IT, Northwestern State University, Louisiana

Savoring words.
ROMEO AND JULIET, Northwestern State University, Louisiana

Lovers and clowns.
THE WINTER'S TALE, Northwestern State University, Louisiana

Rustic, bawdy humor in abundance.
THE WINTER'S TALE, Northwestern State University, Louisiana

Simple communication comes first. **A MIDSUMMER NIGHT'S DREAM,** Northwestern State University, Louisiana

Pomp and pageantry.
AS YOU LIKE IT, Northwestern State University, Louisiana

Two recent "editions" of Northwestern State University's "Shakesperience" Touring Group.

The troupes have promoted Shakespeare and entertained students in eight states and are regular participants in conferences around the country.

At left, the 1999-2000 Troupe.
Below, the 2000-2001 cast.

Skill in stage combat using period weapons.
ROMEO AND JULIET, Northwestern State University, Louisiana

Graceful movement in period costumes.
AS YOU LIKE IT, Northwestern State University , Louisiana

Painting boldly on a broad canvas.
THE TAMING OF THE SHREW,
Northwestern State University, Louisiana

Characters found in extreme circumstances.
MACBETH, Northwestern State University, Louisiana

Utilizing Shakespearean size and technique in musical comedy.
ONCE UPON A MATTRESS, Northwestern State University, Louisiana

Shakespeare musicalized in Spanish Harlem.
WESTSIDE STORY, Northwestern State University, Louisiana

Shakespeare in a different matrix.
AS YOU LIKE IT.   Northern Kentucky University.
Directed by Dr. Jack Wann

Intensity is a hallmark of
Shakespearean performance.
Here applied in a new play, THE BEAST,
Northern Kentucky University,
Directed by Dr. Jack Wann

Unit Seven
SHAKESPEARE: PRESENTATIONAL OR REPRESENTATIONAL
Is the Audience There Or Not?

Let them be well used, for they are the
abstract and brief chronicles of the time.

—Hamlet

REPRESENTATIONAL acting asks an audience to peer into the stage area in the role of a kind of fly on an "invisible fourth wall" and observe the naturalistic behavior of characters in a world created in a play. The modern movement called realism made almost exclusive use of this manner of presentation.

Conversely, PRESENTATIONAL actors acknowledge the presence of the audience, sometimes even interacting with them.

Effective Shakespearean acting calls for BOTH. The audience becomes a kind of ideal "confidante," at times serving as a sounding board for the private thoughts of characters alone onstage or apart from their fellow actors. The actor using this technique talks "to himself" by projecting that other self as God, the gods, evil spirits, Fate, Providence, an absent friend, or even as objects (Macbeth's "is this a dagger I see before me?" or Marc Antony's "Pardon me thou bleeding piece of earth.") Another illustration of this personification of elements is observing the mad King Lear shouting at the storm on the blasted heath. The audience becomes the missing "other" or partner in the scene. This is not "internal dialogue," but is an actual shared moment with an audience that has received an invitation to participate. Shakespeare's plays were performed at two o`clock in the afternoon with 3,000 patrons packed into a space that modern scholars estimate would have been crowded with half that number. The audience surrounded the actors on three sides, they were THERE, and interaction with them was unavoidable.

If the goal of successful acting is to make the audience listen, can there be a better way to do this than to involve them by talking directly to them? They can share in "moments" and combine with their peers to generate common responses. Few joys for actors can surpass the immediacy felt when an audience has been truly reached. This presentational technique provides spontaneous feedback and permits the actor to know if what he is doing is impacting. Unless the performer can achieve what one director called "getting the hook" into an audience so that they can send something back to the stage, he will never really experience what the collaboration between actor and audience can be.

Shakespeare wrote with this kind of immediate and shared experience in mind. In dialogue moments and in scenes, the audience can become surrogates for the others on the stage and experience a sense of sharing. But with monologues and soliloquies, the Shakespearean actor must let the audience "in" somehow. To avoid becoming bored with what John Barton calls "litanies," recited into thin air, (meaning set speeches or soliloquies with no life of their own), audiences must enter into agreement with the actor and become involved like an additional character. The art of theatre is not complete until there is an audience. Even as the actor completes the work of the playwright, the audience may be allowed to complete the work of both.

Barton also warns that soliloquies (especially famous ones) can be treated with too much reverence, making them become the "museum pieces" we warned about earlier. Acting presentationally, in soliloquies, requires a strong sense of the NEED to talk while alone about an issue or circumstance significant enough to have to communicate it to something or someone. The audience, in becoming that "someone," revels in being viscerally involved with how actors cope in a "real" and spontaneous manner. On the other hand, it is certain they WILL become bored if monologues are recited as if they were embroidered on a sampler or quoted at a Kiwanis Club speaking engagement. You must "behave," and behave honestly when you "strut and fret" on the Shakespearean stage. You cannot talk about behavior. Keep it simple and keep it real.

The most important facet of playing without a false sense is to keep your eye on the ball — your objective or intention. Always know what your argument is and what you are fighting for. In this way, actors discover how to share private thoughts honestly.

An illustration of a moment that works well presentationally is one of the great comic situations in all of Shakespeare — the "gulling" of Malvolio in *Twelfth Night*. The vain but gullible lesser court official Malvolio is in the process of being taken in by Maria, Sir Toby Belch and Sir Andrew Aguecheek. He has just found a letter planted by the trio which he believes is from his employer the lady Olivia. A rare opportunity for realization and expansion of an outrageous comic circumstance presents itself if Malvolio is allowed to share, even physically, his ridiculous excitement over the letter with his "confidantes" (the members of the audience) who, of course, already know about the trick.

A PRESENTATIONAL APPROACH

(Do Exercise 9. at the end of this unit.)

In many ways, when the Shakespearean actor soliloquizes, it is similar to performing "in one" in a modern musical comedy. There are, in fact, many similarities between certain aspects of presenting Shakespeare and the style employed in contemporary musical theatre. With a heartfelt message so big that it has to be sung, the character is permitted to pour his or her heart out in musical solos. In Shakespeare's plays, it is often the same. We see a private, significant thought seeking expression. Then, since psychologists have taught us that we are always in a "self talking to self" mode, we discover that making that second party the audience can become a rewarding acting tool.

This would have been the case in Shakespeare's own day, as performances varied greatly from day to day, according to circumstances (such as the makeup and behavior of a given audience — often boisterous, beer-swilling, orange-pelting groundlings— weather conditions, and a variety of ranks and levels of education standing or sitting in close proximity). There was no formal director to control consistency in performance beyond the stage manager/book keeper who monitored the words of the playwright; so actors performed their roles unguided, doing what they could invent to win and to sustain audience attention, approval, and understanding. They HAD to deal with them.

Remember, these plays were performed in the daylight (no moody lighting effects, realistic scenery, or background music aided audience focus and reaction). The actors had to dominate the stage strictly through their handling of WORDS. Keeping it simple, clear and probably, very physical, they almost certainly invited audiences to join them on their journeys of exploration. Responsible only to memorized "sides" (actors were given only their own lines to study), they sought the rewards of performance each time they took the stage by courting the audience (making them their special confidantes) and winning their support. The presentational approach served these circumstances well.

SUMMARY:

    1. Representational acting asks the audience to look in through an invisible fourth wall.

    2. Presentational acting acknowledges the presence of the audience, sometimes even involving them.

    3. Shakespeare uses both, creating a kind of ideal "confidante" to talk to in soliloquies and asides.

EXERCISE 9
THE PRESENTATIONAL MONOLOGUE

(Work Malvolio's comic monologue, treating it as a soliloquy for the benefit of the audience. Actually SHOW them the letter, try to get them to side with you in the assurance that it IS from Olivia and that she DOES possibly love you. Don't make this a strictly male endeavor. It will be fun to see what the ladies do with this material.)

Malvolio: (*Twelfth Night*)

(NOTE: Ellipsis .... indicates comment by the tricksters)

By my life, this is my lady's hand. These be

her very c's, her u's, and her t's, and thus makes she

her great p's. It is, in contempt of question, her hand.

"To the unknown belov'd, this, and

my good wishes": - her very phrases! By your

leave, wax. Soft! And the impressure her Lucrece,

with which she uses to seal. 'Tis my lady. To

whom should this be?

.....

"Jove knows I love,

But who?

Lips, do not move;

No man must know."

"No man must know." What follows? The numbers

alter'd! "No man must know." If this should be thee,

Malvolio?

.....

"I may command where I adore,

But silence, like a Lucrece knife,

With bloodless stroke my heart doth gore;

M,O,A,I, doth sway my life."

......

     "M.O.A.I. doth sway my life." Nay, but first let me see, let me see, let me see.

......

"I may command where I adore." Why, she may command me: I serve her, she is my lady. Why, this is evident to any formal capacity, there is no obstruction in this. And the end- what should that alphabetical position portend? If I could make that resemble something in me! Softly! M,O,A,I,—

.....

M – Malvolio; M – why, that begins my name.

......

M- but then there is no consonancy in the sequel; that suffers under probation. A should follow, but O does.

......

And then I comes behind.

.....

M,O,A,I; This simulation is not as the former; and yet, to crush this a little, it would bow to me, for every one of these letters are in my name. Soft, here follows prose.

(Reads.) "If this fall into thy hand, revolve. In my stars I am above thee, but be not afraid of greatness. Some are born great, some achieve greatness, and some have greatness thrust upon 'em. Thy Fates open

their hands, let thy blood and spirit embrace them, and
to inure thyself to what thou art like to be, cast
thy humble slough and appear fresh. Be opposite with
a kinsman, surly with servants; let thy tongue tang
arguments of state; put thyself into the trick of
singularity. She thus advises thee that sighs for thee.
Remember who commended thy yellow stockings,
and wish'd to see thee ever cross-garter'd: I say,
remember. Go to, thou art made, if thou desir'st to be
so; if not, let me see thee a steward still, the fellow of
servants, and not worthy to touch Fortune's fingers.
Farewell. She that would alter services with thee,

The Fortunate-Unhappy."

Daylight and champain discovers no more. This is
open. I will be proud, I will read politic authors,
I will baffle Sir Toby, I will wash off gross
acquaintance, I will be point-devise the very man.
I do not now fool myself, to let imagination jade me;
for every reason excites to this, that my lady loves me.
She did commend my yellow stockings of late, she did
praise my leg being cross-garter'd, and in this
she manifests herself to my love, and with a kind of
injunction drives me to these habits of her liking.
I thank my stars, I am happy. I will be strange, stout,
in yellow stockings, and cross-garter'd, even
with the swiftness of putting on. Jove and my stars
be prais'd! Here is yet a postscript.

(Reads.) "Thou canst not choose but know who I am. If thou entertain'st my love, let it appear in thy smiling; thy smiles become thee well. Therefore in my presence still smile, dear my sweet, I prithee." Jove, I thank thee. I will smile, I will do every thing that thou wilt have me. (Exit.)

Unit Eight
SHAKESPEARE'S "METHOD"

Will My Current Acting Training Help Me with Shakespeare or Is This a "Whole New Ballgame?"

Though this be madness, yet there is method in it.
—Polonius in *Hamlet*

Nearly all young actors today are trained in Stanislavsky or Stanislavsky-based technique. Since we have observed that there are essentially no stage directions provided in Shakespeare's texts and the concept of the director and of an actor's "character work" come much later in the development of theatre practice; directing/teaching devices such as "subtext" and "given circumstances" would be completely alien to Elizabethan actors. But, whether by instinct or just as a "genius at work," Shakespeare made his plays teem with practical understanding of concepts later formalized in the "Method," the prevalent acting technique of the 20th century.

How could Shakespeare's insights and the "hidden direction" that we have mentioned before foreshadow acting technique brought into vogue 400 years later by the Russian master teacher Constantin Stanislavsky and his followers? Initial observation shows Shakespeare's character's (there were more than 850 of them) circumstances are explored by actors from their own point of view as a member of the Moscow Art Theatre might. This kind of search fits well with the philosophy behind "The Method." But obvious parallels would need to end there. The use of character "motivations," "beats," "units," "objectives," "superobjectives," "emotional memory," and the "subtext" mentioned earlier, would be totally foreign to Shakespeare's approach to mounting a play.

But, consciously or not, Shakespeare did prove a beacon relative to much of what was to happen in the area of acting on the stage in the 20th century. (Sigmund Freud even names many of his case studies after "dramatis personae" in the plays.) This 16th century playwright, like Stanislavsky in Russia many years later, was a rebel against stilted and bombastic approaches to acting that fell short of how people really talked and behaved. Both stated in print that they abhorred artifice and overacting. To this extent, they were kindred spirits.

"Given circumstances" is an illustration of one facet of Stanislavsky's method of study and preparation. Modern theatre practitioners ask actors to be concerned with elements such as environmental circumstances. They question the previous action of the play and what it had revealed, the changes in attitude from the beginning to the end of the "story" of the play (the "polar attitude" or the "arc"), what might be inferred from the dialogue, and what clues can be drawn from the dramatic action itself.

Shakespeare provided no specific environments for his scenes. Locales were often added by scholars or printers long after the Elizabethan playwright flourished. Instructions like "another part of the forest" or "a platform before the castle" are not Shakespeare's inventions. He employs the five-act structure prevalent in Elizabethan England, but he provides no headings for scenes and certainly no environmental cues beyond what the characters say. But they said a great deal and it is not difficult to isolate time and place, not through journeys into "subtext," but from overt textual information or through clues in the dialogue. It is possible to determine geographical location ("in fair Verona, where we lay our scene"), climate ("The day is hot, the Capels are abroad"), time of year (even the day of the week), and season ("At Christmas I no more desire a rose/Than wish a snow in May's new-fangled shows;/But like of each thing that in season grows") from the words provided to the characters. In like manner, economic circumstances, the political environment, and the social and religious conditions so necessary for Stanislavsky's method of preparation are decipherable in Shakespeare from a close examination of the plays themselves.

The circumstances of previous action (what the characters have done and what they have to say about one another) are apparent in the plays. The "arc" we referred to earlier (that is, what changes or remains the same from the beginning to the end of the play) is always a meaningful plot element in Shakespeare. Our friend Malvolio, for instance, does not change at all ("I'll be reveng'd on the whole pack of you") while Macbeth, subjected to a whole series of shifts of fortune, ends his life aware at last of the equivocation of prophecies regarding unholy ambition. This kind of knowledge serves to inform actor choices and decisions about character motivations or goals.

The choice of words, phrases, and sentence structure in the dialogue reveals much. In Shakespeare we have already emphasized the significance of the alternate use of verse and prose. Choice of images, dialect and the overall sound of the text also contribute to a surprisingly modern arsenal for text analysis. This could be, on the surface, consistent with later formal innovation by Stanislavsky. The acting teacher's maxim that the dialogue contains the action and exists only in present tense, "spoken to elicit a response," is as true in Shakespeare's texts as anywhere in the world of dramatic literature.

Although he would never have broken his action into "beats" or "units," Shakespeare's work does lend itself to modern analytical techniques. One can easily discover objectives (even "super" objectives) in the work. A method approach by modern actors to many of Shakespeare's plays proves effective, although the playwright himself would never have dreamed of such an application, any more than he would have understood the psychological and philosophical implications now engendered by his plays. The major difference in the approaches is that Shakespeare's actors required no subtext because the TEXT provided for their needs. For Shakespeare, text and subtext are essentially the same thing, leaving any private or secret musings for asides and soliloquies. Where Stanislavsky put the onus on the actor; Shakespeare wrote it into the text.

In spite of the often dual natures of his "personae," Shakespeare seldom takes sides. In fact, the dramatic conflict in many of his characters rages between two or more elements within the same personality. Who reads *Macbeth* without acknowledging the ambitious tyrant while also recognizing the noble warrior and dutiful husband? This condition of human duality is a constant theme in Shakespeare and provides the impetus for much of the action in the plays. This also explains why the opposites used in the writing carry such import. "It is not what becomes of a man; but what a man becomes" is an adage well-applied to Shakespeare's heroes and heroines. Coming to terms with what are often monumental struggles, Shakespearean characters somehow sustain an affirmative, even life-enhancing spirit. Amidst the chaos that decorates the stage at the end of some of the plays, order has returned on some level. Something good has come of it all. This dramatic philosophy must be comprehended and given consideration if you are to attempt to provide subtextual analysis or application of any other "Method" devices on his text. The language of the text remains the key to everything the actor needs to know and to do. Kenneth Muir has stated that any attempt to turn Shakespeare into a naturalistic dramatist should be resisted. Again and again, in Shakespeare...go to the text!

SUMMARY:
1. Shakespeare and elements of Stanislavsky's "Method" may be complementary.
2. Shakespeare is text-driven. Stanislavsky's methods are actor-driven.
3. Method devices (like "given circumstances") are instinctively in play in Shakespeare, but are never naturalistic choices of the playwright.
4. The dual nature of Man is a key to understanding what undergirds the actions of Shakespeare's dramatis personae.

EXERCISE 10
SHAKESPEARE DONE "METHODICALLY"

Take one of the selections below and approach it from a strictly "Method" angle of analysis. Provide a subtext (preferably different from that in the play) and try to use all of Stanislavsky's techniques that you can recall. Then do a second rendition of the piece using only what the text provides to inform your character choices. See if there is an appreciable difference in where this takes your interpretation and in what develops.

Leontes (*The Winter's Tale*): Inch-thick, knee-deep,

o'er head and ears a fork'd one!

Go play, boy, play. Thy mother plays, and I

Play too, but so disgrac'd a part, whose issue

Will hiss me to my grave: contempt and clamor

Will be my knell. Go play, boy, play. There have been

(Or I am much deceiv'd) cuckolds ere now,

And many a man there is (even at this present,

Now, while I speak this) holds his wife by th' arm,

That little thinks she has been sluic'd in 's absence,

And his pond fish'd by his next neighbor—by

Sir Smile, his neighbor.

Cleopatra (*Antony and Cleopatra*):

Give me my robe, put on my crown, I have

Immortal longings in me. Now no more

The juice of Egypt's grape shall moist this lip.

Yare, yare, good Iras, quick. Methinks I hear

Antony call; I see him rouse himself

To praise my noble act. I hear him mock

The luck of Caesar, which the gods give men

To excuse their after wrath. Husband, I come!

Now to that name my courage prove my title!

I am fire and air; my other elements

I give to baser life. So, have you done?

Come then, and take the last warmth of my lips.

Farewell, kind Charmian, Iras, long farewell.

Unit Nine
THEMES AND ISSUES
What Are Shakespeare's Plays About?

He was not of an Age,
But for all time.

—Ben Jonson

If you act in Shakespeare's plays, your knowledge of the recurrent themes and issues that he addresses will prove significant in your background study. As Jonson says in the famous line above, Shakespeare as a thinker and as a writer is universal and speaks to all men for all time. Pragmatic wisdom and a compassionate humanistic philosophy toward existence illuminate all his writing. Although isolating definitive "topics" is an impossible task, since he has spoken so profoundly on many subjects, it may serve the student actor to highlight several areas that achieve frequent attention in the works. This "top eleven" list names only broad categories, and the themes are arranged in no particular order.

1.

Time's the king of men;

He's both their parent, and he is their grave,

And gives them what he will, not what they crave.

—*Pericles*

TIME is a major theme in Shakespeare's plays. Whether discussing its ravages or its healing aspects, the playwright is often occupied with the concept. The "old common arbitrator," although perhaps most significant in plays like *Troilus and Cressida*, is apparent in some fashion in practically every play Shakespeare wrote.

2.

The DUALITY OF MAN'S NATURE is a second important theme. Whether man is depicted pondering "to be or not to be" or considering alternate and seemingly contradictory courses of action, the exploration of opposites is a common theme.

> This supernatural soliciting
>
> Cannot be ill, cannot be good. If ill,
>
> Why hath it given me earnest of success
>
> Commencing in a truth? I am Thane of Cawdor.
>
> If good, why do I yield to that suggestion
>
> Whose horrid image doth unfix my hair
>
> And make my seated heart knock at my ribs
>
> Against the use of nature?
>
> —Macbeth in *Macbeth*

We often encounter man at odds with himself. The consideration of opposing courses of action and the contemplation of the mixture of evil and virtue that resides in all men are frequent themes. Duality not only becomes an issue, but is in the writing technique as was apparent in the previous section dealing with antithesis and opposites.

3.

> Our remedies oft in ourselves do lie,
>
> Which we ascribe to heaven. The fated sky
>
> Gives us free scope, only doth backward pull
>
> Our slow designs when we ourselves are dull.
>
> — Helena in *All's Well That Ends Well*

The view that REMEDIES ARE MOST OFTEN FOUND IN OURSELVES is a concept brought frequently to bear in the works. Hamlet struggles with the need to realize this as his "inaction" thwarts his designs for revenge.

4.

What is aught, but as 'tis valued?

—Troilus in *Troilus and Cressida*

The VALUE placed on things and the relative attention we give to important issues like love and war is definable only in terms of what weight ("value") we elect to give to them. Shakespeare's characters talked often and at length about this subject.

5.

The ASPIRATIONS OF INDIVIDUALS often come into conflict with religious taboos, governmental and political demands and unbending constraints of their societies. This theme, depicting the pros and cons of civil disobedience, became a frequent theme for Shakespeare. He seemed to conclude that, if characters allow their all-too-human passions to override the dictates of the society in which they dwell, the results may be tragic or even fatal. He does not, however, suggest that the individual should bow to such constraints; he simply demonstrates the possible negative results of such conflicts.

What win I, if I gain the thing I seek?

A dream, a breath, a froth of fleeting joy,

Who…sells eternity to get a toy?

—Lucrece

6.

AMBITION ("hubris" or extreme arrogance) CONTAINS in itself THE SEEDS OF DESTRUCTION. Political ambition is especially portrayed as futile and "bootless" in its results. The Scottish Lord exemplifies this best discovering in the end the nothingness signified by unfettered ambition in his "To-morrow" speech. But the curse of overweening ambition appears in many of the plays.

Fling away ambition.

By that sin fell the angels.

—Cardinal Wolsey in *Henry VIII*

7.

TOO RIGID A SENSE OF JUSTICE, WITHOUT MERCY, will ultimately fall short of its goal. Shakespeare seems to hold all "excessive" personalities suspect and apart from characters who don't like music (beware of them), he holds that mercy must temper all things.

Sweet Mercy is Nobility's true badge."

—Tamora in *Titus Andronicus*

The quality of mercy is not strain'd…

—Portia in *The Merchant of Venice*

8.

FOLLY in high places MUST BE EXPOSED. The welfare of society can only be served if such foibles are not excused, but brought into the light and cleansed. Shakespeare did not suffer fools gladly.

You that are so tender o'er his follies,

Will never do him good.

—Paulina in *The Winter's Tale*

9.

POLITICAL POWER MUST BE USED WISELY. Absolute power certainly can corrupt absolutely in the plays of Shakespeare. This is well depicted in *Measure for Measure* when Isabella reminds Angelo, who is puffing with newfound authority:

O, it is excellent

To have a giant's strength,

but it is tyrranous to use it like a giant."

10.

Men should be what they seem.

—Iago in *Othello*.

This issue of IDEALISM appears mostly in the court-centered plays; but when the individual morality of a central character is pitted against the machinations of running a kingdom or a country, Shakespeare, while championing the courage to speak out, never fails to grant full shrift to the pragmatic requirements of statesmanship. He examines its possible conflict with the position taken by the individual or collection of individuals in the confrontation. He is no "cock-eyed optimist" in all cases. Although Machiavelli was distasteful to him, pragmatic statesmanship could be a subject of admiration.

11.

I find my zenith doth depend upon
  A most auspicious star.

—   Prospero in *The Tempest*

The theme of the POWER OF PROVIDENCE OVER THE TRANSIENT NATURE OF EARTHLY GLORY appears frequently in Shakespeare. The speaker of Sonnet 94 says that "Everything that grows holds on perfection but a little moment." This challenges the grip of transitory power and defers to the authority of the gods, Fate, or Providence.

The issues and themes included here are only a few of those voiced by the some 850 individuals who inhabit Shakespeare's plays, but they do constitute a portion of his "scripture" and wisdom.

SUMMARY: THEMES AND ISSUES

    Time

    Duality in man

    Remedies in ourselves

    Value

    Aspirations of individuals vs.state

    Ambition contains the seeds of destruction

    Too-rigid justice fails without mercy

    Expose folly!

    Use political power wisely

    Hold to idealism, but with caution

    Transient nature of earthly rewards

EXERCISE 11

Select a theme or an issue from the list above. Choose a Shakespearean play or the story of a play that you have heard about and discuss the issues in debate or panel form. Check newspapers and magazines to find parallels. You will discover that there are many "universal" themes that resonate from the 16th century to the present day.

Unit Ten
T.I.P.S.

Tips in the Performance of Shakespeare

Portia: Good sentences, and well pronounced.
Nerissa: They would be better if well-followed.
—*The Merchant of Venice*

Up to this point we have examined classical Shakespearean practice with little attention to the general acting techniques which are already possessed by student actors. There are numerous aspects of what could be called "basic" techniques in modern performance that effectively apply to doing Shakespeare. This unit highlights some basic tenets that speak equally to contemporary acting training and the special demands of Shakespearean text.

At the core of all acting are counterbalanced three essential qualities - the NEED TO BE UNDERSTOOD, the ABILITY TO MOVE and the ABILITY TO READ. A young artist equipped with these three tools can reasonably aspire to enter into the demanding world of theatre practice and to the Elizabethan world of Shakespeare. The word "understanding" as used above, encompasses more than the intellectual comprehension of the material the actor sets out to present. It also defines an artist's desire to communicate knowledge by understanding it at a level high enough to support reasonable expectation of sharing it with others. The capacity to "move well," always a major requirement of theatrical presentation, is never more in evidence than in the mounting of classical work. Specialized movement skills, such as stage combat or dance, (frequently in period costumes) present major challenges. Only determined training and experience can produce the desired results in this arena. But, it is training and experience that is available to you if you choose to go for it. READING both "intensively" into the specific scripts at hand as well as "extensively" into the whole world of literature heads this trio of abilities and is the single most important facet of preparation of any actor, especially one aspiring to epic works like those of Shakespeare.

The skills described so far are needed before one should even consider walking on Goethe's "tightrope" of acting. It is unwise to venture into public performance without an overwhelming need to do so.

But even given these essential abilities, there remain certain expectations that the actor must meet to proceed in this most visceral form of artistic expression.

You must expect to be SEEN; expect to be HEARD; and expect to have auditors (both your onstage collaborators and audience) RESPOND to you. You must want this. Just as you study motivations for your acting, you must bring to the table of performance practice the need to have the audience participate in what you have discovered. You "share the goodies." So if you welcome the challenge of these three facets of actor expectation AND feel you possess the core of abilities mentioned earlier, you may have arrived at a springboard for preparation. You may be said to be equipped for your art.

As suggested earlier, Shakespeare enjoins you to "behave" on stage. You must never strive for some elusive style that you somehow equate with classical acting. Without pretense, you are asked to BE the character (given his rank, education, circumstances, and attitude). It is a fruitless quest to search for some enigmatic "Guru's way" to do this work. This text supports neither the enlightened paths some claim to have found nor the "learn your lines and don't bump into the furniture" methods of the totally pragmatic. If you do attempt to applique some "arty style" on your work, you end up with an affected "recounting" of your lines or an impression of some other artist's efforts. Worse yet, you find yourself "reporting" your lines and thoughts (adding a third person to performance and losing the "I" of the here and now). It is counterproductive to attempt to demonstrate even highly admired behavior onstage; YOU must do the behaving. What works for others may not work for you. You don't play a flute and a tuba the same way. Whether you are a flute or the tuba, allow for the individual differences in the instruments. Shakespeare's text will give you what you need to know to achieve this.

You are asked to have a point of view — a position from which your "argument" (or intention/motivation) may emerge. Given this, you know what you want or are fighting for and you are able to make active choices to attain your goals. This allows you, as an actor to concentrate on "WHAT you are doing" and not "HOW you are doing." One by one, as your intentions become clear, you take them, confronted as they will be by various obstacles, and arrive at the actions that are called for. This journey of decision-making (your active "choices") is the play, during which you as the actor must remain "accessible" and totally open to all that occurs in the text you are attempting to bring to life on the stage. Having determined what each event in the work means to you, what it "costs," or what the stakes may be, you then become free to behave realistically, "acting" in the manner that Shakespearean text demands. Jon Jory used to say, "Raise the stakes and intensify the obstacles." This is the actor approach that will produce the results you seek in a "Shakesperience."

Working always from lively impulses, particularizing all your relationships with both people and the environment of the play, and demanding spontaneous response, you LISTEN AND REACT honestly. This is really all that acting IS- listening actively and responding as a living, breathing, and credible human being.

Earlier, reference was made to the danger of "reporting" behavior in lieu of actually behaving. Other terms that describe this false kind of acting might be "monitoring," "illustrating," or "indicating." These are all forms of the disease of behaving dishonestly. When acting is sincere and "real," it registers mostly in the eyes. It has been said that the eyes are the windows of the soul. This is especially true in live performance. If you listen and respond, your eyes will be consistently involved and alive. False acting is most often revealed in vacant eyes.

Another evidence of uncommitted performance is too little, unnecessary, or distracting movement. Look out for the actor who fails to act from the neck down. Many artists sell their gifts short by trying to do it all with their faces and hand gestures, leaving what was successfully internalized trapped on the inside. These "heady" actors often seem better at talking "about" acting than they are at doing it.

Don't fear to play the opposites in what you encounter. Play the UNresolved issues. They are always the most interesting to the audience. Shakespeare's concerns with duality and antithesis should have made us alert to his interest in these conditions. Avoid all forms of forcing. Actors can call too much attention to their technique and their effort. Shakespearean performance requires ease of delivery-a sense of "belonging up there"-, not appearing to be dressed in "borrowed robes." Audiences can be readily put off by the abrasive insistence of actors who try too hard to please.

Some words to the wise are appropriate here. First, work constantly to avoid any regionalism that may creep into your delivery. You certainly don't want a phony sound, but clear, Standard English is your goal. (Don't go for a Richard Burton impression.) Avoid using stereotypical dialects to suggest eccentric characters like rustics or fops. These are not "hillbillies" or "sissies," but are unique to the worlds of their particular plays. Finally, don't anticipate in your performance. Foreshadowing that has a dramatic purpose is effective, but don't pre-play cards that haven't been dealt yet. It will muddy your performance and confuse the audience. (So often, productions of *Romeo and Juliet* illustrate this, shouting out from the first spirited brawls, "We're gonna die, we're all gonna die!") Don't be guilty of this. Let things happen as they happen. Romeo and Juliet is really one of Shakespeare's better comedies until things go awry. Don't play the end at the beginning.

Actors speak of "discoveries" and "realizations." Seek these as you work. Earnestly explore for what the character "finds out" in the course of the action AND allow him the exercise of putting together elements in the plot and realizing what they portend.

There is much advice that could be included in a section called T.I.P.S., but it is hoped that what has been included proves uniquely relevant to early experiences with Shakespeare. Don't make doing Shakespeare harder than it is. These are "real" people placed in intense situations. Don't try to superimpose profundity on the way they behave. Let them respond honestly and directly. As Olivier playfully pointed out when asked what King Lear was really like: "He's like us all really, he's just a stupid old fart."

This may sound frivolous here, but it is the truth. As actors we do not know many King Lears to observe; but we could readily think of a number old "farts" who have behaved stupidly who might lead us to a characterization of this "foolish, fond" old man. In short, when you are unable to draw from your own experience, seek out appropriate models to study and become their advocate.

SUMMARY: T.I.P.S.

1. Be understood. Read and move well.

2. Want to be seen, heard and responded to.

3. Behave. Don't try for some elusive "style."

4. Have a point of view.

5. Listen and react.

6. Avoid reporting and all its relatives.

7. Play the UN-resolved.

8. Avoid regionalisms.

9. Don't foreshadow in performance.

10. Look for discoveries and realizations.

EXERCISE 12

You may not quite understand what "reporting" sounds like. Using the following monologue, try to REPORT the content much in the manner of a contemporary news anchor person. Then, re-analyze the text and decide what you as the speaker are "arguing." Do the monologue again, this time playing the intentions that you determine are correct for the choice you have made. Allow for moments of discovery and realization wherever you may find them.

Chorus (Romeo and Juliet):

Two households, both alike in dignity,

In fair Verona, where we lay our scene,

From ancient grudge break to new mutiny,

Where civil blood makes civil hands unclean.

From forth the fatal loins of these two foes

A pair of star-cross'd lovers take their life;

Whose misadventur'd piteous overthrows

Doth with their death bury their parents' strife.

The fearful passage of their death-mark'd love,

And the continuance of their parents' rage,

Which, but their children's end, nought could remove,

Is now the two hours' traffic of our stage;

The which if you with patient ears attend,

What here shall miss, our toil shall strive to mend.

Unit Eleven
SONNETS

Not marble, nor the gilded ornaments of princes,
Shall outlive this powerful rhyme.
—Sonnet 55

What are sonnets? They are fourteen-line meditations in verse. They were very much the rage in Shakespeare's time, and all serious artists probably had examples of these "thoughts in action" secreted away. They were not intended for publication and if shared at all, were probably shown exclusively to fellow "wits" or other intellectuals capable of appreciating the personal content of the writing.

Structurally, a Shakespearean sonnet consists of three "quatrains" (four lines of verse each in iambic pentameter) followed by a couplet, which serves as a kind of "capper" or summarizing statement to the poem.

An illustration of a typical Shakespearean sonnet is Sonnet 18:

Shall I compare thee to a summer's day?

Thou art more lovely and more temperate:

Rough winds do shake the darling buds of May,

And summer's lease hath all too short a date;

Sometime too hot the eye of heaven shines,

And often is his gold complexion dimm'd,

And every fair from fair sometime declines,

By chance or nature's changing course untrimm'd:

But thy eternal summer shall not fade,

Nor lose possession of that fair thou ow'st,

Nor shall Death brag thou wand'rest in his shade,

When in eternal lines to time thou grow'st.

So long as men can breathe, or eyes can see,

So long lives this, and this gives life to thee.

This familiar selection is only one of some 154 outpourings attributed to Shakespeare. The sonnets are especially useful to actors because they inherently have no plot. Sonnets require the reader to assume a persona, grasp a dilemma, and resolve it in fourteen lines. This generates a wonderful acting exercise. The question of the autobiographical or personal nature of the sonnets is immaterial. For actors, only the content matters. You have fourteen lines to take a position, argue it, and resolve it in the last couplet.

Often the subject matter of the sonnet was love; but other topics abound in these meditations by Shakespeare. There are musings on poetic theory. He even questions himself as a poet. Career and the adversities of Fortune are frequent topics. The passage of Time and the proximity of Death are also frequent subjects for the poet's attention.

Although his attitudes toward friendship are not consistent, it is often considered, both in its changing moods and in the author's gratitude for affection reciprocated. Sometimes his outbursts approach childish, paranoid levels when he tries to come to terms with jealousy, separation (even through Death), and envy.

As to objects for his musings, most often his sonnets speak of three particular personas- a mistress, a rival poet, and a young "friend." A case might be built that the majority of the sonnets are, directly or in veiled fashion, linked to this trio. Vacillating from forgiveness to angry recrimination, the speaker is seen at times on almost impossible "highs" and at other times grovelling in self-loathing.

There is no real evidence as to the identity of some of these objects of affection or loathing. But it is stimulating to conjecture with figures like the young Earl of Southhampton and the mysterious "Dark Lady" as veritable gardens of scholarly delight. However, for acting purposes, you must look only at the sonnets themselves. By imposing arguments, we can provide an actor's intention to these accessible, short dramatic outbursts and can find great pleasure and opportunity for growth in them.

The sonnets can also serve to assist us with the display of "unembarassed emotion" discussed in Unit Three. Provocative subject matter ranging from humiliation, fear of rejection (as actors we may relate to this), self-hatred, gratitude for affection, to all forms of "cries from the heart" supply us with a wealth of material to fashion for ourselves as classroom performances or in private rehearsals.

It is tempting to delve into the content of the sonnets, but that is not our present goal. The inclusion of the sonnets is to allow student-actors to gain appreciation for their value as short performance pieces which allow for a wide variety of interpretation and are not tied to any set locale or circumstance. Make them your own.

EXERCISE 13

Take the following sonnet and perform it from three viewpoints. A. As Shakespeare. B. As you yourself wondering if your best friend is "up to something" with your girl or boyfriend. Or C. As an actor weighing the rigors of the profession against a good "civilian" job.

> Two loves I have of comfort and despair,
>
> Which like two spirits do suggest me still:
>
> The better angel is a man right fair,
>
> The worser spirit a woman color'd ill.
>
> To win me soon to hell, my female evil
>
> Tempteth my better angel from my side,
>
> And would corrupt my saint to be a devil,
>
> Wooing his purity with her foul pride.
>
> And whether that my angel be turn'd fiend

Suspect I may, yet not directly tell,

But being both from me, both to each friend,

I guess one angel in another's hell.

Yet this shall I ne'er know, but live in doubt,

Till my bad angel fire my good one out.

—Sonnet 144

Unit Twelve
WARMING UP TO SHAKESPEARE
Preparation for Rehearsal and Performance

For my voice, I have lost it with hallooing,
and singing of anthems.

—Falstaff in Henry IV (Part 2)

Your body and your voice are your "instruments." Both must be adequately prepared for the rigors of rehearsal and performance. Just as an athlete cannot perform effectively while "cold," neither can the actor. Baseball pitchers begin with a few easy tosses, swimmers begin with comfortable, undemanding leisurely strokes, and actors must find techniques for making a transition into full-blown working form. You must be loose, warm, and ready to work. Failure to do this can result in vocal or bodily injury, pulled muscles, or a diminished ability to respond when the physical and vocal demands of the Shakespearean text are encountered.

Warming up is a personal thing. Some artists require several hours of yoga, EST, "body trips," or other rituals to bring themselves to performance level. Others require considerably less. There is a wonderful story, probably apocryphal, of the Italian opera legend, Ezio Pinza, appearing in Rodgers and Hammerstein's *South Pacific*. After allowing co-star Mary Martin to engage in her lengthy warm-up regimen, he was reported to have stared deeply into his makeup mirror and intoned the words "South Carolina" three times, then walking onto the stage totally ready to perform. It is obviously different for every actor.

Warming up can be subdivided into fewer than a dozen categories or phases. All performers should begin the process with some form of personal preparation or transition into the world of work and out of the routine of daily life. This puts the "civilian" world behind you. There are many ways to do this, including a simple act of will, or concentration. But it must be done. You cannot bring outside problems into your art. Make that transformation from your role as the waitress at Ellen's Stardust Diner to Rosalind in the Forest of Arden. Although physical and vocal warm-ups are equally important, the focus of what follows emphasizes the vocal element. Although both are involved, your own personal approach to the bodily side of your preparation will be respected and your method of getting physically ready to work left to you or to your directors, teachers and fellow-actors.

Once prepared, the first area of concern must be relaxation. Getting rid of tension can be achieved by any number of "tense and release" exercises like " rag dolls," "stacking" vertebrae and diverse forms of "shake-outs." These are mainstays of an actor's training. This unit does not include specific exercises, but rather indicates KINDS of exercise which will help you to achieve your needs in each step of the warm-up process. What you do and how you do it will vary with personal preferences and physical condition.

Once you are relaxed, the next area for attention is breathing. Some simple form of taking in air and controlling exhalation, followed by intakes with modulation (like "ahhh" sounds or blubbers) on the exhale serve nicely for this step. Diaphragmatic breathing involves pushing the abdomen OUT when inhaling and pulling it IN when exhaling. Stay aware of this pattern for breathing throughout your warm-up.

Ordinary humming can be a valuable step in an effective preparation for work. Using five to six count patterns, hold on to a vowel sound and let it resonate. Good phrases for this exercise are "Down and Out," "Now and Then," "Who are you?" "Me and Mine," "Here today, Gone tomorrow," "a loud sound," or "a round tone." Once you have done several of these, start the phrases again and begin to "chew" on them as if they were tangible and tasty.

After humming, some form of singing and intoning should follow. Select a familiar ditty, and sing it without effort bouncing around on various pitches (pitches are the frequency of the vibrations of the vocal cords) to establish some optimum levels for your voice. Chanting is also useful at this stage of the warmup. Good resonation is achieved when you sense a liquid, comfortable flow of air over your cords. Intoning, chanting, resonating, and singing are variations on a similar theme, but all four have separate and specific value in the warm up. Make them each a part of your routine.

Now comes the time to articulate. The lips, the tongue, the palate and the oral cavity all need to be brought into play. The work of Gilbert and Sullivan, Dr. Seuss, Edward Lear, and Lewis Carroll have all proved pleasant and profitable sources of articulation exercises. Definitely, include a series of words in your warm-up that contain the consonant sounds of English. For example:

Babe	Hah!	Pope	Wow!
Cake	Judge	Roar	Zinc
Deed	Lull	Shush!	
Fife	Maim	Tut	
Gag	Nine	Verve	

After working the vowel sounds and the articulators, you should feel ready to project. You should not have attempted anything "full voice" prior to this stage of your preparation. It is distressing that many young actors think "warming up" is leaping immediately to this level, shouting out projected phrases without doing anything to prepare for them. This would prove as counterproductive as the baseball pitcher walking out to the mound and starting to throw 100 mph fastballs stone-cold.

Projection involves the application of force and energy. Some of the best projection has little to do with volume. Richard Burton, playing in *Equus* on Broadway, "whispered" his long speech describing Dysart's envy of young Alan. That memorable monologue filled every nook and cranny of the theatre. Force and energy!

You may want to interpret— to "act" a bit— as you come to the end of your warm-up routine. Remember that interpretation encompasses both intellectual and emotional goals. Work on both in this final phase of your preparation to rehearse or perform. It is probably best to use material from the play in which you are currently employed. If you have made your transition into the working world of the rehearsal or performance, relaxed, worked on breath control, hummed, sang, intoned, sought resonation, articulated, projected, and finally interpreted, you have provided yourself with an effective warm-up. It doesn't take much time at the various levels, but each of the categories deserves attention and will produce results.

Your personal approach is ultimately the best for you, but do consider what has been included above as potentially useful in the process. Above all, don't try to go on with no preparation. The pulled muscle that may result could be your career.

SUMMARY:

     1. Preparation

     2. Relaxation

     3. Breath control

     4. Humming

     5. Singing

     6. Intoning

     7. Resonating

     8. Articulating

     9. Projecting

     10. Interpreting

(These should be done in sequence. Don't move to one until you have completed the other.)

EXERCISE 14

Here are several exercises to help you warm up your voice. Do these with an over-articulated, even silly vocal approach. Have fun with them.

A.   What do you know about tweetle beetles?
     Well.. When tweetle beetles fight, it's called a tweetle beetle
     battle.
     And when they battle in a puddle, it's a tweetle beetle puddle
     battle.

B.   Then the feathers popped out! With a zang! With a zing!
     They blossomed like flowers that bloom in the spring.
     All fit for a queen! What a sight to behold!
     They sparkled like diamonds and gumdrops and gold!
     Like silk! Like spaghetti! Like satin! Like lace!
     They burst out like rockets all over the place!
     They waved in the air and they swished in the breeze!
     And some were as long as the branches of trees.
     And STILL they kept growing! They popped and they popped
     Until, long about sundown when, finally, they stopped.

C.   Painting pink pajamas.
     Policemen in a pail
     Peter Pepper's puppy.
     And now
     Papa's in the pail.

     Four fluffy feathers
     On a
     Fiffer-feffer-feff

     Silly Sammy Slick
     Sipped six sodas
     And got sick, sick, sick.

D.   Moses supposes his toeses are roses,
     But Moses supposes amiss,
     For Moses he know his toeses aren't roses
     As Moses supposes his toeses is.

Around the rugged rock the ragged rascal ran.

Chop, chop, choppety-chop,
Chop off the bottom and chop off the top,
What there is left we will pop in the pot,
Chop, chop, choppety-chop.

D. Now entertain conjecture of a time
When creeping murmur and the pouring dark
Fills the wide vessel of the universe!

F. To sit in solemn silence in a dull, dark dock,
In a pestilential prison with a life-long lock,
A-waiting the sensation of a short, sharp shock,
From a cheap and chippy chopper on a big, black block!
From a cheap and chippy chopper on a big, black block!

Continue to explore Dr. Seuss, Gilbert and Sullivan, Edward Lear, and Lewis Carroll (for example, "Jabberwocky") for dozens more challenging vocal gymnastics.

Unit Thirteen
THE TWELVE COMMANDMENTS
Some Suggestions Regarding "Life in Art"

"Faster than spring-time showers comes thought on thought."
—Richard of York in *Henry VI*

Regardless of curses on The Scottish Play and the absence of thirteenth floors in many downtown New York hotels, a Unit Thirteen has found its way into this book. However, for fear of tempting Providence too much, the section will be limited to a kind of "Ten (We'll opt for Twelve) Commandments" for those actors preparing for a "Shakesperience."

THOU SHALT STAY REALLY HEALTHY!
Shakespeare Sez: " There's nothing ill can dwell in such a temple."

Your body is indeed your "temple." Take care of it. No matter how talented you are or how motivated you may be, if you bring a sick or tired body to the classical stage, you risk failure. The physical and emotional demands of Shakespearean performance are just too great to accommodate fragile or sickly participants.

THOU SHALT BE UNIQUE!
Shakespeare Sez: "He was a man, take him for all in all:
    I shall not look upon his like again."

No one else is like you! Welcome this. Be proud of it. Project your own thoughts and your personal view of the world. Theatre people are considered "off horses" in many circles anyway, and those who work in the classics would be rated "way off." But remain that unique human being that you are and joyfully undertake the challenges of the art and the lifestyle that you have chosen.

THOU SHALT HIE THEE TO THE GYM!

Shakespeare Sez: "Our bodies are gardens, to which our wills are gardeners."

Exercise should be a regular part of your daily life. A daily routine of swimming, fencing, tennis, or dance should be given priority. Shakespearean actors fight with various weapons, dance the gavotte and the minuet with equal skill, and leap about the stage as supernatural beings. This calls for a body "at the ready" and able to do what you ask of it. Work out and treat your instrument well. The violinist would not dream of deliberately beating his instrument against a wall. You should have the same respect for the condition of your voice and body. Smoking, screaming at the football game, and venturing into the cold without a scarf are examples of foolish mistreatment of your instrument.

THOU SHALT EAT RIGHT!

Shakespeare Sez: "Unquiet meals make ill digestions."

A diet of Twinkies and Dr. Pepper will not provide the sustenance to support a classical actor. Find ways and time to enjoy good meals. The performance of a play by Mr. Shakespeare is at least the equivalent of a full-length NBA game with Mr. Jordan.

THOU SHALT NOT KEEP THY FELLOWS WAITING!

Shakespeare Sez: "I wasted time, and now doth time waste me."

There is probably nothing more important than promptness. Don't be guilty of wasting the time of others. Be early, appropriately dressed and ready to work. If each member of a 30-member cast of The Scottish Play were five minutes late, the result would be almost two and a half hours of wasted time. Punctuality is professionalism. It is something that you have complete control of if you choose to exercise that control. Do so.

THOU SHALT LEAVE PERSONAL PROBLEMS "TO HOME."

Shakespeare Sez: " A poor player, That struts and frets his hour upon the stage, And then is heard no more."

Borrowing the advice of the Emcee in "Cabaret," leave your problems "outside." There is no room for personal problems in art. The "strutting" and "fretting" you are called upon to provide must come from the soul of the character. If you carry your personal life onto the stage, you crowd out the potential for exploring the life of the figure you portray. The less room for "you," the more room for artistic transformation. All focus must go to the classroom project, the rehearsal, or the performance.

THOU SHALT NOT ALLOW THY ENERGY TO FLAG!

Shakespeare Sez: "Great men tremble when the lion roars."

If this work is not the most vital thing in your life, get out of it and find something that does excite you. Make room for the people who really care. Enjoy it! Acting is a privilege and a joy. Treat it as such by drawing upon all the resources you have.

THOU SHALT NOT BADMOUTH THE USHERS!

Shakespeare Sez: "I hold the world but as the world, Gratiano, A stage, where every man must play a part...."

Theatre is a collaboration. Everyone does have a part to play. You must respect your colleagues—all of them. Hopefully, you are all on the same page, striving to do a good play well. Everyone connected with the project has an equal opportunity and responsibility for bringing this about. Allow room for conflicting ideas and for group endeavors to be nurtured. There are no problems in the theatre, only projects.

THOU SHALT DO THY HOMEWORK!

Shakespeare Sez: "Study what you most affect."

Tranio's advice in *The Taming of the Shrew* is especially sound in the preparation period for a production, the time designated for studying your role. The actor must never trust only his memory. Write down important thoughts in some form of journal. Keep written versions of all notes that teachers, directors and stage managers give you at the end of class or rehearsal.

Allow specific time outside the rehearsal hall for re-thinking your work.

Bring something "newly minted" to each and every session. How many times has a director cried out in anguish, "Bring me SOMETHING!"

THOU SHALT NOT PLAY "PRISSY!"

Shakespeare Sez: "Is black so base a hue?"

Don't be afraid to get dirty. You will get cut and bruised, roughed up, tired and dirty playing Shakespeare. You'll be the victim and the perpetrator of accidents. You will have to show monumental patience with peers. But through it all, bear in mind that the hands-on work in the shops and the heads-in-gear work on the stage cannot exist without one another. So, when it's time to use your head, use it; and when it's time to pitch in and get dirty, do it. All leads to the same destination- a great show.

THOU SHALT CHAMPION RIGHTS AND RESPONSIBILITIES ALIKE!

Shakespeare Sez: "I have in equal balance justly weighed
What wrongs our arms may do, what wrongs we suffer,
And find our griefs heavier than our offences."

No one is in the theatre to serve anyone else. Everyone has a job to do and no job is secondary. Let others do their work. Whether in a high school show or a professional production, expect, even demand your rights. By the same token, live up to your responsibilities. This dichotomy of rights and responsibilities is often observed in productions of Shakespeare's plays where cast members and crews are diverse in their experience with classical literature and the often monumental building demands. Be patient and "suffer" any wrongs gamely, hoping that your own offences have not outweighed them. ACTORS DO HAVE RIGHTS AND RESPONSIBILITIES. Expect, even demand your professional rights; but live up to the responsibilities with equal vigor.

Unit Fourteen
THE MATRIX

Is It Nobler in the Mind to Carry Audiences Backward in Time
or Propel Playscripts Forward?

> But pardon, gentles all,
> The flat unraised spirits that have dar'd
> On this unworthy scaffold to bring forth
> So great an object. Can this cockpit hold
> The vasty fields of France? Or may we cram
> Within this wooden O the very casques
> That did affright the air at Agincourt?
>
> ...ON YOUR IMAGINARY FORCES WORK.*
> Piece out our imperfections with your thoughts;
> Into a thousand parts divide one man,
> And make imaginary puissance;
> Think, when we talk of horses, that you see them
> Printing their proud hoofs i' th' receiving earth;
> For 'TIS YOUR THOUGHTS*that now must
>   deck our kings,
> Carry them here and there, jumping o'er times,
> Turning the accomplishment of many years
> Into an hour-glass: for the which supply,
> Admit me Chorus to this history;
> Who, Prologue-like, your humble patience pray,
> Gently to hear, kindly to judge, our play.
> —Prologue, Henry V

Here Shakespeare flat-out tells us how to approach his plays. He challenges US to work on our "imaginary forces." He asks US to participate fully in the "experience" of his play- OUR "Shakesperience."

*Author's Capitalization.

Our responsibility, in turn, is to transmit his challenge to our audiences. We must, as Francis Hodge has put it, "move others to move others." But, How? The question emerges, "Should we bring that script up to date or travel backward in time with the audience?" Given verse, archaic language, overbold staging, and all the daunting elements in the plays, are we not forced to do one or the other? The answer is "No." Shakespeare's response suggests we do "neither AND both." He has relieved us of the decision to tackle historical gymnastics as we try to define words that are no longer in use and play elaborate charades with perplexed playgoers. He provides an easy out for our "bootless" efforts at rewriting scripts in order to cater to contemporary taste and comprehension. Simply do neither. The dramatized truths contained in the soaring beauty of his language make it unnecessary to "time travel" backwards or to "update" to reach audiences. His "word images" do what no amount of adaptation or doctoring can achieve. The universality of Shakespeare's language will continue to attract and hold audiences for as long as dramatic literature is performed.

Why can we not expect contemporary audiences to "entertain conjecture of a time" when a beautiful silken flag went up a pole on top of a playhouse just across the Thames? It was a time when playgoers left work early or ditched school to load the boats and barges that would take them over the river to "their" theatre. They readily laid down their one, two or three pennies, according to the dictates of their pocketbooks. Such a price was reasonable to them, and there were few complaints about spending money for an "afternoon's enchantment" during which they might enjoy singing, dancing, slapstick, and swordplay as well as poetry, passion, politics and philosophy (often framed in language that was as new to them as it is to us today). A bargain!

If we time travel, we can see the actors, often attired in splendid costumes (albeit hand-me-downs from wealthy patrons) readily identifiable as carpenters or kings, magicians, ghosts, monsters, or fairies by the way they are dressed. But no lights and no backdrops are there to assist us. The environs, the moods, the colors, even the smells were created by one single artistic element, Shakespeare's language, those "word images." THIS is why he is so universal. His value will never depend on any "matrix" and does not require audiences to be culturally bound to the themes of the plays. It is in the words. This is why you can set the plays anywhere and do them in almost limitless fashion over unending decades…because the "play IS the thing."

To transport audiences back to those days would require a broad education. Glossaries, footnotes, program notes, pre-show panels, post-show discussions would need to be provided and would soon test the endurance of the staunchest playgoer. It mustn't be done this way. Educate, yes. But educate through exposure. Take the advice given to actors: let audiences learn by immersion. They will. Look at the history of Shakespearean performance. They already have!

They gain added exposure through modern adaptations, good or bad. This "popularizing" compounds the staying power that Shakespeare still enjoys over the years. In fact, most student actors are not even too put off by bad productions. There are faulty productions of the work of every playwright since Sophocles. But if they keep trying to climb Mt. Shakespeare, perhaps they know that there is something there to strive for. Be eager to applaud any effort at any level (recall the artisans of *A Midsummer Night's Dream*?). Why do you suppose that the children's theatre companies of Shakespeare's own time and the hundreds of English schoolboy productions of Shakespeare in the past century that nurtured the Oliviers of this world were so popular?

But, just as attempts to take audiences backward in time fail, so too much updating can also prove disastrous. Certainly, the actor may choose to use a dagger gesture when he says the word "bodkin" and he can pour imaginary liquid from a "bombard" to show his audience what the words mean; but this falls into the realm of help, not necessity. Many directors actually change the words. You can do this, attempting to sustain meter or disregarding it, but you risk doing damage to proven material. In short, adapt with care. Good Shakespearean actors have learned to use inflection, facial expression, and gesture for clarity and to make their intentions lucid. "Never and Always" collaborate with Shakespeare. But in interpreting a script, don't assume the role of a new creator. Never let go of your responsibility for interpretation of the playwright's words.

So, a matrix is really up to you. Set it in Spanish Harlem, on an island in World War II, in the "Wild West," or on a "Forbidden Planet." Shakespeare's genius has allowed you that kind of latitude. And if you are clever, you will succeed AS LONG AS YOU RESPECT THE WORDS. The matrices are boundless, but only when you don't get "cute" with the source of Shakespeare's universality—his language.

Strive to educate your audiences AND to train yourselves as actors and directors to use every device at your disposal to clarify and make accessible the words of the most respected playwright in the English language. It's worth any amount of effort. What an artistic adventure it is to go searching for treasure when you know full well it's there to be discovered and enjoyed.

EPILOGUE

Bringing Our Revels to an End

As transparently romantic as the intention may be, this book ends with one of the most famous Shakespearean speeches in all literature. Prospero, a mighty white magician, is putting his affairs in order. He will return to a life of politics and statesmanship after a term of exile on an island. He has learned much about himself and the ways of the real and the supernatural world.

> Our revels now are ended. These our actors
>
> (As I foretold you) were all spirits, and
>
> Are melted into air, into thin air,
>
> And like the baseless fabric of this vision,
>
> The cloud-capp'd tow'rs, the gorgeous palaces,
>
> The solemn temples, the great globe itself,
>
> Yea, all which it inherit, shall dissolve,
>
> And, like this insubstantial pageant faded,
>
> Leave not a rack behind. We are such stuff
>
> As dreams are made on; and our little life
>
> Is rounded with a sleep.

> —Prospero in *The Tempest*

You students and aspiring young actors are the "all" who inherit the "stuff that dreams are made on." Shakespeare took us far beyond a "little" life in showing us the "tow'rs, palaces and temples" of his profound imagination. We are obliged to take our inheritance, and especially "the great globe itself" — our art—seriously.

Selected Bibliography

Armstrong, Jane (Compiled). THE ARDEN DICTIONARY OF SHAKESPEAREAN QUOTATIONS. London: Thomas Learning, 2000.

Asimov, Isaac. ASIMOV'S GUIDE TO SHAKESPEARE. New York: Wing Books, 1970.

Barber, C. L. SHAKESPEARE'S FESTIVE COMEDY. Princeton, N.J.: Princeton University Press, 1959.

Barton, John. PLAYING SHAKESPEARE. London/New York: Metheun, 1986.

Berry, Herbert. SHAKESPEARE'S PLAYHOUSES. AMS Studies in the Renaissance, no. 19, New York: 1987.

Berry, Ralph. ON DIRECTING SHAKESPEARE. London: Hamish Hamilton, 1989.

Bevington, David. THE COMPLETE WORKS OF SHAKESPEARE. New York: Harper et al., 1992.

Bloom, Harold. SHAKESPEARE-THE INVENTION OF THE HUMAN. New York: Riverhead Books, 1998.

Boyce, Charles. SHAKESPEARE A TO Z. New York/Oxford: Roundtable Press Book, 1990.

Bradley, A. C. SHAKESPEAREAN TRAGEDY. London: Penguin Books, 1991.

Brine, Adrian and Michael York. A SHAKESPEAREAN ACTOR PREPARES. Lyme, N.H.: Smith and Kraus, 2000.

Brubaker, E. S. SHAKESPEARE ALOUD. Lancaster, PA, Published by the Author, 1983.

Bullen, A. H. et al. THE WORKS OF WILLIAM SHAKESPEARE. New York: Oxford University Press. 1939.

Burgess, Anthony. SHAKESPEARE. Chicago: Ivan R. Dee, 1994.

Cahn, Victor L. SHAKESPEARE, THE PLAYWRIGHT. Westport, CN: Praeger, 1996.

Campbell, Oscar James and Edward G. Quinn. THE READER'S ENCYCLOPEDIA OF SHAKESPEARE. New York: MJF Books, 1966.

Chambers, E. K. THE ELIZABETHAN STAGE (Four Volumes). Oxford: Clarendon Press, 1923.

Chute, Marchette. AN INTRODUCTION TO SHAKESPEARE. New York: Scholastic Book Services, 1951.

_____. SHAKESPEARE OF LONDON. New York: E.P. Dutton Co., Inc., 1949.

Cohen, Robert. ACTING IN SHAKESPEARE. London/Toronto: Mayfield, 1991.

Craig, Hardin. AN INTERPRETATION OF SHAKESPEARE. New York:
Dryden Press, 1948.

Cross, Wilbur L. and Tucker Brooke (gen.ed.). THE YALE SHAKESPEARE. New York:
Barnes and Noble, 1993.

Dawson, A. B. SHAKESPEARE IN PERFORMANCE: HAMLET. Manchester and
New York: Manchester University Press, 1995.

Epstein, Norrie. THE FRIENDLY SHAKESPEARE. New York: Penguin, 1993.

Evans, G. Blakemore (text ed.) THE RIVERSIDE SHAKESPEARE. Boston: Houghton
Mifflin, 1974.

Fiedler, L. THE STRANGER IN SHAKESPEARE. New York: Stein and Day, 1972.

Goldman, Michael. ACTING AND ACTION IN SHAKESPEAREAN TRAGEDY.
Princeton, N.J.: Princeton University Press, 1985.

Granville-Barker, Harley. PREFACES TO SHAKESPEARE, Vol. 1. Princeton, N.J.:
Princeton University Press, 1975.

_____. PREFACES TO SHAKESPEARE, Vol.2. Princeton, N. J.: Princeton Univer-
sity Press, 1975.

Greenblatt, Stephen et al. (Gen. Ed.). THE NORTON SHAKESPEARE.
W. W. Norton and Company, 1997.

Gurr, A. PLAYGOING IN SHAKESPEARE'S LONDON. Cambridge: Cambridge
University Press, 1996.

Hamilton, Charles. IN SEARCH OF SHAKESPEARE. London: Robert Hale, 1986.

Harbage, Alfred (Gen. Ed.). WILLIAM SHAKESPEARE; THE COMPLETE WORKS.
New York: Viking, 1977.

Harrison, G. B. SHAKESPEARE: THE COMPLETE WORKS. New York:
Harcourt, Brace and Co., 1952.

Honigmann, E.A.J. SHAKESPEARE: "THE LOST YEARS." Manchester:
Manchester University Press, 1985.

Joseph, Bertram. ACTING SHAKESPEARE. New York: Theatre Arts Books, 196

Knight, G. W. THE WHEEL OF FIRE. London: Metheuen, 1949.

Levi, Peter. THE LIFE AND TIMES OF WILLIAM SHAKESPEARE. London:
Macmillan, 1988.

Levin, Bernard. ENTHUSIASMS. London: Cape, 1983.

McDonald, Russ, ed. SHAKESPEARE REREAD. Ithaca, N.Y.: Cornell University Press, 1994.

Muir, Kenneth. SHAKESPEARE CONTRASTS AND CONTROVERSIES. Norman, OK: University of Oklahoma Press, 1983.

_____. THE SOURCES OF SHAKESPEARE'S PLAYS. London: Metheun, 1977.

Partridge, Eric. SHAKESPEARE'S BAWDY. London: Routledge, 1947.

Proudfoot, Richard (Gen. Ed.). THE ARDEN SHAKESPEARE. New York: Metheuen, 1976.

Rowse, A. L. SHAKESPEARE'S SONNETS. New York: Harper, 1964.

_____. WILLIAM SHAKESPEARE: A BIOGRAPHY. New York: Harper and Row, 1963.

Saccio, Peter. SHAKESPEARE'S ENGLISH KINGS. New York: Oxford, 1977.

Schoenbaum, S. SHAKESPEARE'S LIVES. New York: Oxford University Press, 1991.

_____. WILLIAM SHAKESPEARE, A DOCUMENTARY LIFE. New York: Oxford University Press, 1975.

Sitwell, Edith. A HANDBOOK ON WILLIAM SHAKESPEARE. New York: Beacon Paperbacks, 1961.

Sobran, Joseph. ALIAS SHAKESPEARE. New York: The Free Press, 1997.

Spurgeon, Caroline F.E. SHAKESPEARE'S IMAGERY. Boston: Beacon Press, 1960.

Turgeon, Thomas S. IMPROVISING SHAKESPEARE. New York: McGraw Hill, 1981.

Vendler, Helen. THE ART OF SHAKESPEARE'S SONNETS. Cambridge, MS: Belknap Press, 1997.

Warren, R. STAGING SHAKESPEARE'S LATE PLAYS. Oxford: Clarendon, 1990.

Whalen, Richard F. SHAKESPEARE-WHO WAS HE? Westport, CN: Praeger, 1994.

Wilson, J. Dover. THE ESSENTIAL SHAKESPEARE. London: Cambridge University Press, 1978.

_____. WHAT HAPPENS IN HAMLET. London: Cambridge University Press, 1935.